MOBILIZING APPROP|

This publication is based on a seminar held in
Oslo in March 1987. The seminar was sponsored by
**THE ROYAL NORWEGIAN MINISTRY OF DEVELOPMENT
CO-OPERATION**
and was organized by
the Norwegian Society of Chartered Engineers' Associated
Group on Developing Countries.

MOBILIZING APPROPRIATE TECHNOLOGY

Papers on Planning Aid Programmes

Vesla Vetlesen   George McRobie   John White

Sven A. Holmsen   Paul Hofseth   Marit Melhuus

Iftikar Ahmed   Marilyn Carr   Steinar Skjaeveland

Edited by MATTHEW S. GAMSER

IT PUBLICATIONS 1988

Intermediate Technology Publications Ltd,
103–105 Southampton Row, London WC1 4HH, UK

© Intermediate Technology Publications 1988

ISBN 1 85339 045 3

Typeset by J&L Composition Ltd, Filey, North Yorkshire
Printed in Great Britain by The Short Run Press, Exeter

CONTENTS

Preface

THE NORWEGIAN SOCIETY of Chartered Engineers' Associated Group on Developing Countries, in conjunction with the Royal Norwegian Ministry of Development Co-operation (MDC), organized a conference on 'Appropriate Technology in the Norwegian Development Assistance Programme', held in Oslo from 24-5 March 1987. The conference was held in conjunction with ITDG's 'Design for Need' exhibition. The conference objectives were:

o to enable participants to examine the concept and implications of Appropriate Technology, and the extent and manner in which these concepts are being applied in bilateral and international aid programmes,
o to examine Norway's current Development Assistance Programme in light of the above, and to consider the extent and manner in which the programme might be adjusted to meet the strategic objectives incorporated in the concept, and
o to inform, motivate and encourage participants to examine how they might introduce more appropriate technologies for developing countries within their own programmes and activities.

Some eighty-nine people took part in the proceedings, including representatives from Norwegian government agencies, universities, private companies, and invited lecturers from the Intermediate Technology Development Group, the International Labour Organisation, and the Organisation for Economic Co-operation and Development. As the conference provided much time for the discussion of the major presentations and workshop sessions in small, issue-oriented discussion groups, it was possible to profit greatly from the diverse backgrounds and interests of the assembly.

Seven formal presentations were made on various aspects of Appropriate Technology (AT) and its use in development assistance. These and the opening and closing addresses are presented in full in this volume. While it is not possible to record all the groups' discussions in their entirety, they were a vital part of the conference, and this writer here endeavours to present the major issues they raised during this two-day period.

Much of the discussion surrounded the relation of Norwegian technical assistance to the 'project cycle', the stages through which a technology moves from the initial identification of needs to widespread production and use (see Marilyn Carr's presentation for a more detailed discussion of this topic). There was concern that much Norwegian aid was not entering this cycle at an early stage, and therefore had limited influence over the technology choice, and limited contact with those grassroots organizations that play a key role in development and change in rural areas. The advancement of alternative, more appropriate technologies requires action at the initial needs identification and investigative stage. The successful development and dissemination of these technologies requires a closer collaboration with local groups responsible for rural productive activities, particularly with women's organizations.

It was also pointed out that the project cycle itself needed to be changed to make it more flexible in adapting technologies to accommodate local resources and needs. Designs, plans and methods must often be adapted as a technology moves from pilot to wider production and use, but projects are often not able to change course when these needs for adaptation are identified. Development assistance has to modify its own procedures to make such mid-cycle adjustments possible. Better monitoring and evaluation methods, too, are required to keep abreast of project effects and impacts, and to indicate in a timely fashion when adjustments are necessary.

At the same time, the advancement of appropriate technologies requires more 'macro' level work with governments and multilateral donors to bring about changes at the policy level to make these technology options more attractive. Developing country governments often resist alternative technology choices because they lack 'prestige'. If Norway wishes to disseminate labour-intensive road construction methods and similar, more appropriate options, it should make a policy statement to this effect and should use the evidence from successful pilot efforts to persuade LDC policy to support these efforts.

Several of the presentations and comments concerned the meaning of Appropriate Technology. It was pointed out that 'technology' is more than machines and tools, and that a critical aspect of 'appropriateness' is the productive and sustained use of new practices and products. Technical assistance should include provisions for training local people how to operate and maintain technologies. Also, the role of social scientists in technical assistance has to be made more prominent and more constructive. They need to take a more active part in shaping projects, and not just be used to identify potential problems with already-developed project plans. A more 'interactive' project planning should develop, which takes a broad and long-term view of local needs and conditions, and makes better use of local knowledge and resources. In addition, planning should take better account of the environmental implications of the introduction of new technology.

The work of the five discussion groups enabled the participants to delve more deeply into various aspects of appropriate technology and its role in development assistance. The groups began by considering short issues papers, which raised some of the questions and dilemmas facing Appropriate Technology development (these are listed in the Appendix). The debates were both lively and productive, enlarging upon some of the major themes introduced by the speakers.

Group 1 considered why the Norwegian Government aid programme did not have a better awareness of Appropriate Technology and its potential. Norway's small population, its lack of a colonial past, and its inexperience with the problems of economic recession all were felt to hinder a greater understanding of Appropriate Technology. There was, however, a significant body of knowledge present in the form of the collective field experiences of Norwegian aid workers. The group urged that better use be made of this capacity through improved communications within this aid community, and that government should make a clear policy commitment (involving specific objectives, funds, people, and time) in support of the greater development of Appropriate Technologies.

Group 2 examined alternative approaches to Appropriate Technology development. It was decided that a bias in favour of either the rural or the urban poor was not a good idea, as the poor from both areas need help. Two principal technology development strategies were identified: extension-based methods, suited to most health, education, and public utility projects; and commercial strategies, more suited to small-scale, income-generating projects such as food processing operations or 'hardware' distribution and services. Commercial methods also can be used as a follow-up for ventures emerging from initial extension efforts. The strengthening of local organizations has to be an essential part of both approaches. Also, more attention should be given to supporting small-scale industries, through developing national advisory and finance bodies geared to their needs, and through the more effective dissemination of information about appropriate technologies at the grass-roots level.

Group 3 looked at the effects and the impact of Appropriate Technology development. It pointed out that a project can benefit some groups at the expense of others (men vs. women, consumers vs. producers, adults vs. children, etc). There need not always be 'losers' from development aid, but careful planning needs to be done to ensure that the immediate gains of a small group are not made at the expense of the longer-term welfare of the larger body of an area's poor, or of the environment. In addition, the continuous monitoring of a project's effects, particularly its generation of local income, is needed to enable plans to be adjusted as practical experience is gained.

Group 4 discussed how various institutions can support Appropriate

Technology development. Many different bodies can be involved in this process, including universities, R and D institutions, commercial companies, banks, government bodies, non-government organizations (NGOs) and international agencies. It was remarked that greater use needs to be made of local NGOs and of local knowledge, particularly women's knowledge. Much more work could be done in organizing those various institutions to work together in developing and promoting appropriate technologies. The potential is there, but in Norway, for the moment, it remains largely untapped.

Group 5 analysed the issues arising in the transfer of technologies. It was decided that this process should consist not primarily of an exchange of fixed products, but rather of a development of indigenous technical capacity, and knowledge of how this capacity could be put to use in introducing new technologies. Far more emphasis needs to be given to the role of training in this process, and to the skill and personnel requirements for the maintenance and sustained operation of new systems. Technology designs need to be flexible, to adapt to local needs and capabilities. The group felt that the 'software' aspects of technology deserved greater attention.

As the meeting progressed, the discussion turned more and more to the question of how the Norwegian Development Assistance Programme itself should handle the development of Appropriate Technology. It was pointed out that this is a time of opportunity, as old solutions are being scrapped and new ones explored. Norway has many institutions involved in Appropriate Technology work, including universities, professional societies, research institutes, private firms, MDC and NORAD. There was, however, no vehicle for collecting and sharing the valuable knowledge and experience available as a result of these initiatives.

A suggestion was made that a Norwegian 'focal point' for Appropriate Technology be established. This would provide a centre for enquiries from all groups interested in trying out new approaches in development assistance as well as a source for Norwegian policy statements on the role of Appropriate Technology in the aid process. It would also serve as a point of contact between domestic researchers and grass-roots organizations in developing countries, to help in needs identification and the establishment of new research direction.

Several participants urged that this 'focal point' not become a completely new institution, but should be built into an existing organization. There was no general agreement as to what specific institutional changes would best provide this new service for Appropriate Technology development, but there was general consensus that, due to the limited size and scope of Norway's development assistance work, the new body should concentrate on those technology areas which it emphasizes. MDC's on-going research programme on technology transfer should provide it with important information and support in this regard.

As one participant noted, the new body should bring Appropriate Technology more into the mainstream of Norwegian development assistance, and not 'put it in a box off in the corner'. The key to making Appropriate Technology work in Norwegian aid is to increase communication about its potential and its effects, both among Norwegian institutions, and between them and grass-roots organizations in developing countries.

The consensus, as expressed by Mr Skjaeveland of MDC in his closing address, was that the time is ripe for changes in technology and development assistance, and that this opportunity should not be let pass by. Greater communication and greater participation should be emphasized in project design and technology choice, in order to bring about development that is sustainable over the long term. Norway already has much experience in Appropriate Technology work, but it needs to put its knowledge into wider availability, so that more people both at home and overseas can benefit from it.

Matthew S. Gamser
Policy Planning Unit, ITDG

Opening address

VESLA VETLESEN
*Minister, The Royal Norwegian Ministry of
Development Co-operation*

ANY DEVELOPMENT has to start somewhere; it starts not only with the situation today, but also with conditions based on development in the past. Development is dependent to a large extent on our ability to learn from our deeds and mistakes.

Norwegian development assistance started twenty-five years ago.

The twenty-fifth anniversary will be celebrated later this year. In the life of a human being twenty-five years make you an adult; in a historical perspective twenty-five years is not that much. Nevertheless a quarter of a century should have given a generation of people certain experience and certain knowledge about development co-operation.

What does this experience tell us? It tells us over and over again that we cannot step outside the framework within which the projects and the programmes are going to be implemented.

This framework is formed by several components, and among these are terms of trade, and the burden of debt carried by the country in which the co-operation takes place (resulting in convertible currency). The framework also consists of local conditions: social patterns, traditions; technological level; and the availability of raw material and spare parts. (No one who has ever worked in a developing country has avoided being confronted by the problem of lack of spare parts.)

When Norway started development co-operation, this was a new field for us. But many other donor countries, like Great Britain, France and the Netherlands, were also facing a new situation in the Third World. Further, among international organizations experience was also limited: UNDP, for example, was established as late as 1965.

Considering this situation world-wide, as well as in Norway and in the developing countries, nobody should be surprised that mistakes have been made; but we have to learn, and avoid making the same mistake twice. There is a saying: 'Making mistakes will never make you rich, but will make you wise.'

Mutual setting of development targets
Experience and wisdom have made us somewhat more humble and careful. The approach, methodology and technological level of development programmes will have to be reviewed continuously so that it can

be adapted to the development of the co-operating countries or agencies. All parties involved have to participate in discussing and setting the targets for a programme, and thereafter give their contribution in achieving the goals. This process is difficult, and the success of a programme can never be guaranteed in advance.

The technological level of the Western world has developed relatively slowly: from horse cart to the jet plane; from the hand plough to the combine; from the wheelbarrow to the truck. This development is considered as progress and an advantage to mankind. Worldwide, man struggles for a higher level of technology, in the developing countries, as elsewhere. Worldwide, the adoption of high technology is often considered as a scale of their success towards a more developed society. This fact puts heavy pressure on governments in the Third World — and on donor countries as well!

In addition, in the developing world high- and low-cost technology are being applied side by side. The commercial farmer is using a combine while the small-scale farmer next door is using a hand plough. The social tension is obvious, and makes the decisions, on the technological level, even more complicated.

The understanding of technology in a developed and a developing country is difficult to compare, but it is of vital importance that we try to understand and accept the developing country's way of thinking and acting. Otherwise, it will be almost impossible to contribute to genuine development.

The creation of a Movement
During the last twenty years we have experienced a growing awareness of problems which are vital to the future of mankind: population growth; pollution of environment; the exhaustion of natural resources; the economic imbalance between North and South.

These problems were put on the agenda and several organizations were established; it was in this context that the terms 'intermediate' and 'appropriate' technology (AT) were created.

What is Appropriate Technology (AT)?
There are many definitions of the term AT. The question of appropriateness is left for Mr McRobie. The Project group for this seminar has obviously a wide understanding of AT. AT is far more than a technological level between hi-tech and low cost technology; it takes into account the economic conditions; ecology and the environment; natural and other resources locally available; human resources development, including community participation and women's involvement. Thus it could be said that AT is a way of adapting to those experiences which I men-

2

tioned initially, developing within the given framework, taking into account the limits and utilizing the possibilities.

Welcome
I am pleased to see and address this audience of people committed to development aid. It is of great value that the participants come from different backgrounds like industry, consultancy, research institutions and authorities.

The organizers of this seminar, the Ministry of Development Cooperation with the Norwegian Society of Chartered Engineers and the Associated Group on Developing Countries, would like to give a special and warm welcome to our friends from England — the Intermediate Technology Development Group. ITDG is a non-profit organization, of approximately the same age as NORAD. As can be seen in the exhibition, and will emerge during the seminar, the ITDG staff has extensive experience in applying Appropriate Technology in developing programmes. The seminar and in particular the exhibition would have been impossible without their contribution.

With these words, and by wishing all the participants and visitors a hearty welcome, I declare the exhibitions and seminar opened.

Technologies for developing countries: what is appropriate?

GEORGE McROBIE
Vice-President ITDG

Consider the auk;
Becoming extinct because he forgot how to fly, and could only walk.
Consider man, who may well become extinct
Because he forgot how to walk and learned how to fly before he thought.
Ogden Nash

FUTURE HISTORIANS will, I believe, agree that one of the misfortunes of the poor of the world was that the industrialized countries started to take an active interest in Third World development in the middle of the twentieth century. Fifty years earlier, or fifty years later, the technologies that would have been transferred from the rich to the poor countries would have been very different from those of the 1950s and 1960s; and ideas about what constitutes 'development' would probably have been very different too. Certainly the technology of the early 1900s, both in industry and agriculture, would have been more labour-intensive and thus more appropriate to Third World needs than the highly complex and vastly expensive contemporary technologies; and if we look fifty years ahead, who can doubt that, with the oil-based economy nearing its end, we shall have adopted more sustainable production methods. By the very fact of being sustainable they would be more appropriate than the fossil-energy-intensive technology of industry and agriculture today, which, although very productive, certainly does not have much of a future.

The fact remains, however, that economic development did not become a universal objective until after the Second World War. And from then on, and indeed until quite recently, a prevalent notion of economic development was that cheap and abundant energy and rapid technological progress had opened up an era of limitless and potentially world-wide economic growth. Few questioned the survival value of an economic system based squarely on the heedless exploitation of people, the environment, and the world's stock of non-renewable resources, or doubted the wisdom of advocating its adoption by the then newly independent countries of the Third World.

It was in relation to the needs and resources of the developing world

4

that the deficiencies of rich-country technologies first became evident. The critical role of technology in economic development was first brought into focus by E.F. Schumacher in the early 1960s. He argued that Third World countries were relying on rich-country technologies at their peril; that the large-scale, capital- and energy-intensive industries of the rich countries would do more to exacerbate than to solve the problems of the poor countries. Such technologies were singularly inappropriate because they:

o offer relatively few, very expensive workplaces, whereas the poor countries, with their masses of un- and under-employed, desperately needed very large numbers of relatively inexpensive workplaces;

o are located chiefly in cities, which offer the mass markets, scarce skills and infrastructure facilities not found in rural areas where the majority of the poor live;

o in many instances, compete out of existence traditional non-farm activities formerly carried on in rural areas;

o accelerate the migration of people from rural areas to metropolitan centres;

o make the developing country increasingly dependent upon rich countries for spare parts, skills and, often, markets;

o distort the cultures, as well as the economies of poor countries by concentrating economic activity in cities and social élites, breaking down rural structures (technology is not culturally neutral).

In 1965 a group of us helped Schumacher to start the Intermediate Technology Development Group in London. Our starting point was the belief that mass unemployment and rural misery could be overcome only by creating new workplaces in the rural areas themselves; that these workplaces must be low-cost so that they can be created in very large numbers without calling for impossible levels of savings or imports; that production methods and associated services must be kept relatively simple, and that production should be largely from local materials, for local use.

While it was (and still is) conventional in the field of development to put quite undue emphasis on GNP as a measure of success, the Group was informed by the knowledge that development basically means the development of people — their education, organization and discipline, and their access to and control of the tools and equipment with which they can work themselves out of their poverty.

Our purpose was to demonstrate that technologies appropriate to the needs and resources of the rural poor could be developed and introduced, and then, by helping to create an international network of like-minded organizations, to change the whole emphasis of aid and development towards small-scale technology suitable for rural development, a technology really capable of bringing industry into the rural areas.

5

At first, and for several years, the Group did not get a very warm welcome either in rich or in poor countries. But then the conventional strategy of development, based on large-scale capital intensive industries, came to be increasingly challenged by development economists and planners. Many of the large industries proved to be very inefficient, kept going only by protection and subsidies. They did not generate the hoped-for surpluses and they did nothing to raise the living standards of the majority, the rural and urban poor.

Although conventional wisdom, as J.K. Galbraith has observed, is very slow to change, by the mid-1970s the accumulating evidence of the failure of the large-scale industry strategy was accompanied by the long overdue recognition that small-scale, localized industry and agriculture can reduce transport costs, decelerate city growth, produce goods and services very efficiently, and are the best way of distributing incomes. Then came the failure of African argiculture; the vast and unrepayable Third World debt; and the relentless growth of unemployment in developing countries. These largely man-made, disastrous developments, served to underscore the fact that encouraging the poor to behave as if they were already very rich only compounds their problems.

Because most poor people in the world make a living by working on small farms, in small family businesses or as artisans, technologies appropriate to their needs and resources will generally be small, relatively simple, inexpensive and (to be sustainable) non-violent towards people and the environment. But experience has shown that it is not by any means enough to produce and field-test such technologies. Devising or adapting the right hardware is part of a package which includes identifying the specific needs and resources of the community; developing a technology that can meet their needs — that raises their real income on a sustainable basis; and getting the technology widely introduced under operating conditions. Obviously, to be appropriate, the technology should be capable of local operation and maintenance, and local or at least indigenous manufacture, it should be owned and operated by its users, and result in a significant increase in their net (real or money) income; it should utilize to the maximum extent local and renewable raw materials and energy and it should lend itself to widespread reproduction using indigenous resources and through the medium of local markets.

An international network
There are, today, at least twenty AT organizations around the world with a significant capacity for identifying needs and undertaking practical research and development work. In the industrialized countries there are the pioneer organizations, ITDG, VITA, Brace Research Institute, more recently joined by AT International, TOOL in Holland, GATE in

6

Germany, GRET in France and IDRC in Canada. Among international organizations, UNICEF and the ILO are major supporters of AT work in developing countries.[1]

Within the developing countries there are now hundreds of AT organizations, ranging from technical R and D groups at one end of the spectrum to information-networking teams at the other.

Thus today, over a wide range of human activities, especially those related to basic human needs, technology choices are becoming available. Small-scale, low-cost technologies now exist in agricultural equipment and food processing, water supply, building materials, textiles, small-scale manufacturing, energy, and transport. What is now beyond question is that technology choices can be created for all practical purposes, across the board; and twenty years' experience in this field has convinced me that when high-quality engineers turn their minds to devising small-scale, capital- and energy-saving technologies, they can produce some remarkable results.[2]

More R and D needed

Yet many gaps in knowledge remain, and the funding of R and D in Appropriate Technology is derisory in relation to the need. For the developing countries the creation of hundreds of millions of new workplaces in agriculture and industry during the next couple of decades is now an overwhelming necessity. It should be one of the most urgent tasks on the agenda of aid-giving governments and international agencies to ensure that at the very least, the technologies enabling a basic needs strategy to be implemented should be readily available to the governments and people of developing countries. This calls for a major expansion of R and D and field testing of, and the publication of data on, appropriate technologies. The impending energy crisis in many poor countries alone requires much additional work on these lines on renewable energy. And every developing country should possess an indigenous AT organization capable of advising government of the technology choices available and of the economic and social implications of different choices, advising on the implementation of AT programmes, and undertaking R and D and technology adaptation to local conditions.

Another area of AT work where much more effort is needed is in the setting up of programmes and projects to establish, on a much wider scale than has yet been done, that ATs are commercially viable and economically sustainable; that raising the productivity and incomes of the rural poor is a good investment all round.

Conditions of success

As yet, relatively few appropriate technologies have spread widely, although many more have achieved local success. Appropriate

7

Technology International has recently compiled the first of a series of detailed case studies entitled, 'High-Impact Appropriate Technologies', [3] which include these examples:

Mark II handpumps in India. The Mark II deep-well (18 to 50m) handpump is now the basis of widespread community water supply in India. More than 600,000 are installed, serving 120–150 million villagers. Some 38 firms employing 8,500 people are now engaged in making these pumps at the rate of about 156,000 a year. Some 50,000 people are employed in well drilling, or the maintenance of existing installations. At village level there is a pump caretaker equipped with a set of tools; at sub-District level, there are roving mechanics; at District level, mobile maintenance teams. The per capita cost to the users (covering the well, pump and maintenance costs) is less than $1 a year. During the past five years, an estimated 15,000 to 20,000 pumps have been exported.

Implementing organizations are UNICEF, the Government of India, State governments, villages and communities, private and public pump manufacturers.

Oral Rehydration Therapy. This is a simple, inexpensive and effective way of treating diarrhoea. Over the past fifteen years ORT has spread to virtually every developing country, and about 100 million packets of ORT sales are produced and distributed annually. There is a growing number of local production units in developing countries, and a home preparation of a basic unit is now envisaged.

Implementing agencies are UNICEF, Red Cross, WHO, government and non-government health services, communities and families.

Water-pumping windmills in Argentina. About 60,000 water-pumping windmills are currently in use in Argentina, and annual production is 1,500 to 2,000. About 300,000 people benefit by getting water for their livestock, and for their own use. The windmill is closely modelled on a standard US multi-blade machine, with rotor sizes of from 6 to 16 feet; and it is now being exported to the USA.

Implementing agencies are private manufacturing companies.

Bamboo-reinforced concrete water tanks, Thailand. More than 24,000 tanks have been installed since 1979. Villagers contribute their labour, pay materials' costs and a small surcharge into a revolving loan fund. Up to 10,000 more tanks are likely to be built in the next three years.

Implementing agencies are Community Based Appropriate Technology and Development Services; some funding from ATI, Ford Foundation, IDRC and CUSO.

Bamboo tubewells, India. Work on bamboo tubewells started in 1967. Since then they have been introduced on a large scale. By 1980 there were some 100,000 wells in Bihar and Uttar Pradesh. A mobile pump services 5 or 6 tubewells, which operate at depths of 30 to 36 metres; work is now in hand on a bullock-powered pump. The technology was developed by farmers and small contractors. Its cost is one-third to one-half that of steel tubewells.

Implementing agencies are Deen Dayal Research Institute, the governments of Bihar and UP, and local entrepreneurs.

Rural Access Roads Programme, Kenya. An example of the AT approach applied to civil engineering. Competitive with capital-intensive methods, the programme established more than 40 field units and completed some 7,000 kilometres of rural roads. It incorporates a technical service unit and a training programme, and employs about 8,000 labourers.

Implementing agencies are the Kenyan Ministry of Transport, IBRD, ILO, and British and other bilateral donors.

Women's Pappad Processing Co-operative Enterprises, India. Started 25 years ago when seven women invested 80 rupees in a low-cost nutritional snack food venture. Today the business generates sales of 30 million rupees and provides income for more than 6,000 co-op members. Raw materials are bought in bulk and distributed to the co-operative's 21 centres, which operate with a good deal of autonomy, and are run entirely by women.

Implementing agency is Lijjat Pappad Women's Co-operative.

Rural small farm implements components manufacture, Tanzania. A decentralized approach to the production of ox-drawn implements (ox carts and toolbars) for small farmers. Two small factories are in production and two others are planned. In two years more than 2,000 ox carts and 2,500 toolbars have been sold. The equipment pays for itself in a matter of months rather than years, as it enables more land to be cultivated. Surveys indicate that only a small fraction of the demand for this equipment has yet been met.

Implementing agencies are Tanzanian public and private implement manufacturers, and USAID.

Other projects with similar potential are not hard to find. Some of the more striking examples that I have come across recently include the local manufacture of fibre-reinforced roofing tiles, an ITDG project in Kenya. From a pilot project of ten production units this is envisaged as 50 production units after four years. By then, local income generation from the project would amount to 2 million Kenyan shillings annually. Low-cost, local manufacture of FCR roofing tiles has potential in practically every developing country. Another example is the small-scale, locally-made *sorghum and millet dehuller*, developed and funded by the International Development Research Centre of Canada in

9

collaboration with several African countries. Some 35 dehullers are in commercial operation in Botswana, 40 are planned in Zimbabwe, 10 are working in the Dominican Republic, and pilot schemes are starting in India and Gambia.

A programme which is well past the pilot stage is ITDG's introduction of *plywood fishing boats* in south India. At least 2,000 fishermen are earning a good living from 400 plywood boats operating along the southwest coast of India. There is now a firm base for a decentralized, capital-saving, skill- and labour-using industry there, for boat-building and repairs. (It should be added here that it is far better to 'unroll' a huge mango tree into plywood which can make many boats, than to use the same tree to make one dugout canoe and a heap of wood chips!). To cite one of the 20 projects of AT International, the introduction of a *small oil press and associated equipment* to small farmers in Cameroon is likely to raise their incomes by at least 50 per cent. This project demonstrates the 'package' character of successful rural projects. It includes a locally-controlled revolving fund which both finances the production of the equipment and enables groups of local farmers to buy it. The farmers first lease the equipment, then purchase it out of their increased incomes.

What are the conditions of success of appropriate technologies of this kind?

First, the technologies themselves have been thoroughly field-tested and refined before going into production: the history of handpump failures is impressive, for example, and tens of thousands of man-hours have been spent on getting animal-drawn equipment right. The technologies lend themselves to local manufacture wholly or in part, and to local maintenance; and they are low cost enough to be afforded by individuals or working groups of the 'target' population.

Secondly, the users or beneficiaries of the technologies are closely associated with the processes of selection, introduction and use of the technology or product; and from the standpoint of the users, the advantages (in the form of cash or higher real income or life enhancement) significantly outweigh the costs incurred by them.

Thirdly, the technologies are disseminated through the mechanism of the market; but in practically every case the market alone would be inadequate – it has to be supplemented in several ways. Thus R and D and testing are preconditions of a product making its appearance in the market. But neither its appearance, nor detailed information about it, puts it in the hands of the rural poor. The poor have no money, or none to spare; their needs must be translated into effective demand, that is demand backed by purchasing power. This requires that the poor have access to credit enabling them to buy the new equipment. They can then, as in the case of the oil-press in Cameroon, repay the loan out of the increased incomes they get by using the new technology. Credit that enables the poor to become more productive lies at the very heart of the process of rural development, of capital accumulation and income generation in rural areas.

Careful attention must also be given to such matters as quality control, training, extension and demonstration, and the creation of new local institutions to ensure continuity of user control and benefit. In all instances, that is, the hardware part of the technology is part of a package which empowers local people to choose what suits them best; gives them access to a low-cost, good quality product over which they have a good measure of control; and which enables them, by using it, to raise their standard of living. Essentially this is investing in people by making them more productive.

The most important reason for the widespread adoption of these technologies is that they have either had support at government level, or that they have in some way overcome or by-passed the formidable obstacles that inhibit ATs in most developing countries. These are familiar enough: development strategies based on top-down, large-scale programmes and projects, and financial policies, administrative procedures and rules that favour the big over the small, the urban over the rural, the rich over the poor. If such obstacles could be lowered or removed, the disastrous consequences of the conventional large-scale technologies would be clearly revealed, and cost-effective ATs would be widely adopted through the market. A thorough exploration, and exchange of national experiences, of ways in which a policy environment favouring ATs (or removing the obstacles to them) is overdue, and is another area of AT activity where more work and support is required.[4]

Education and training have a pervasive role in all the stages of AT work, from the identification of needs through to dissemination, and here again new inputs are required for an AT-based strategy of development to be successfully carried through. New or re-oriented programmes of education and training need to be set up, for scientists and engineers, administrators, planners, field workers, and local people with the intellectual and practical ability required to carry through AT programmes, and the appropriate education and training facilities both in the rich and poor countries are thin on the ground.

It is, of course, in the developing countries that major programmes of education and training in AT should now be built up. Some of the institutions already active in this field have international reputations.[5]

Strengthening existing courses and launching new ones, both in the industrialized and the developing countries, so as to create a really sizeable cadre of men and women proficient in the tasks of implementing AT programmes and projects in developing countries should become a significant part of bilateral and international aid and development effort.

The AT approach, then, has already proved to be an efficient, cost-effective alternative to conventional, largely ineffective, aid and development programmes. What is now needed, to summarize my argument, is a major expansion of R and D effort, field testing and demonstration of AT, supported by enlarged education and training programmes, the creation of local credit and other facilities enabling the poor to get access to, own and operate, new technologies; and the removal of administrative and institutional barriers to the spread of appropriate technologies through the market.

Aid and Appropriate Technology: multilateral and bilateral assistance programmes

JOHN WHITE*

Development Co-operation Directorate, OECD

In 1981, THE ILO produced a working paper, written by myself in collaboration with Fred Fluitman of the ILO staff, on the ways in which aid agencies affected the choice of technology in the projects that they financed. An updated version, with more recent examples supplied by the ILO, was published in 1985.[1]

The working hypothesis of the paper, largely confirmed by the extensive interviews that we undertook in a number of aid agencies, was that the procedures of aid agencies are such as to suppress the choice of technology as a major issue in aid-financed activities. The limitations of the study precluded fieldwork in developing countries in support of the hypothesis, though this was envisaged as a possible next step. Meanwhile, there was plenty of material to hand derived from our general experience as observers of aid. All aid specialists, whether they are in principle in favour of or opposed to aid, have a catalogue of 'horror stories' in which things have gone badly wrong. Two recurring features of these horror stories are failure to assess the characteristics and interrelationships of the intended beneficiaries — often characterized as the social and cultural aspects of development — and failure to explore technological choices in project design. Since the latter takes place in the context of the former, the two are not unconnected.

Within the ILO, there was a tendency to assume that any technological bias in the activities of aid agencies was specifically attributable to the presence of certain practices, notably the practice of tying procurement to the donors' goods and services. Certainly one can find examples in which tying of this sort has had a deleterious effect. The general consensus among aid specialists, however, is that the worst effects of

*The author is on the staff of the Development Co-operation Directorate of the Organisation for Economic Co-operation and Development (OECD). The paper draws heavily on the work of the Expert Group on Aid Evaluation of the OECD's Development Assistance Committee, together with earlier work undertaken for the ILO. The views expressed, however, are put forward by the author in his personal capacity, and do not necessarily reflect those of the OECD or its members, or the ILO.

tying relate to prices rather than to design, and there is currently much concern over this issue because of the growing element of commercialism in some donor's aid programmes. The problem can be largely resolved, however, if donors concentrate on those activities in which they have long experience and comparative advantage. More worrying to aid specialists, as reflected in the aid literature, has been the practice of making aid available only for the import component of projects, since this does indeed impart a bias, in favour of capital-intensive designs which largely exclude small-scale indigenous and often well-proven technologies. Here, however, there has been substantial progress. Members of the OECD's Development Assistance Committee (DAC) subscribe to a set of guidelines on the financing of local and recurrent costs,[2] and the statistical evidence, though patchy, suggests that such financing is now much more freely available than it was.

The Fluitman and White paper was concerned with a much more insidious and pervasive bias. Our observation was that certain key stages in the project cycle were governed by procedures which were largely automatic, causing the question of choice of technology to be overlooked at those points in the cycle when it should in principle have been most visible. The two most conspicuous examples were procurement, where standard procedures were at that time applied, by bilateral and multilateral agencies alike, irrespective of the special features of each case; and the appointment of consultants and other project staff, where procedures ranged from casual contact through reliance on self-description by consultancy firms, to excessive reliance on formal professional qualifications.

Standardization of procedures is partly a matter of bureaucratic convenience, partly, and more significantly, a reflection of accountability. Multilateral agencies are accountable to their member states, in the sense of having to show that procurement is not biased in favour of particular sources; and bilateral agencies are accountable to legislatures. In both cases, investigations with an audit function are easier to meet if it can be demonstrated that an agreed set of rules has been observed. Most agencies in fact have waiver powers that they can exercise in appropriate cases. Although there has been some progress in recent years, it remains significant that these waiver powers are seldom fully used, the most likely explanation being that officials are unwilling to incur the extra work involved in making a case. It should also be noted that current concerns over the growing commercialization of aid programmes have led to a search for procedures which will increase the 'transparency'

14

of transactions with a commercial element, a trend which could give rise to a reversion to the rigidities of the past.[3] On the positive side, it would seem that the most promising course for aid agencies would be to increase assistance aimed at building up the procurement capacity of developing countries themselves — perhaps making use of third countries which already have such capacity, notably India — but assistance of this kind has so far not been energetically promoted by either side. The tendency among most aid recipients, especially the least developed countries, is to remain passive in the face of an assumption that the rules are the rules.

The Fluitman and White paper made a distinction between broad and narrow approaches to the choice of technology as an issue in project design. The narrow approach leads typically to the appointment of a special unit, perhaps just a single adviser, and the identification of a small number of projects as having the choice of technology written into the design, often on an experimental basis. The broad approach, in principle, leads to the setting up of procedures for screening all projects, so that the choice of technology does not escape from the design of projects in which it is significant, merely because nobody thought of it. The general view is that a narrow approach may be necessary, at least in the initial period when an issue such as the choice of technology is still struggling for recognition; but that in the longer term a broader approach, too, is required. It is noteworthy that in certain agencies with long experience of particular sectors the choice of technology has evolved naturally as an issue to be taken into account across the board, having entered into the consciousness not just of someone called a 'technology adviser' but of all the engineering staff responsible for the sector concerned. The case of rural roads is perhaps the most conspicuous in which this process has taken place.

The issue is best handled in the early stages of project appraisal and design. It is procedurally much more difficult to pick up by means of the monitoring processes which most donors apply to project implementation, since at that stage it will entail a modification of a design that is already agreed. The choice of technology, however, is only one of many issues that need to be taken into account in project appraisal and design, and the problem is how to ensure that it is given some prominence at least in those cases where it is most important.

The issues which aid agencies take into account in project appraisal and design can for the purposes of this paper be divided into three broad categories.

First, there are issues which are relevant to virtually all projects. Most but not all of these are now incorporated into the standard

15

procedures of all but a handful of aid agencies, at least where capital projects are concerned. (In technical co-operation, the appraisal process tends to be looser, partly because of problems of measurement.) It would be a brave desk officer today who put forward a case for a project without even an attempt to estimate the economic rate of return, unless he could show explicitly why it was not relevant. Social aspects, similarly, are increasingly taken into account, in the sense that the tendency is to isolate specific categories of project as being less sensitive to social factors — port development, for example — rather than seeing social aspects as something to be considered only in exceptional cases. An issue which is increasingly recognized as having been neglected in the past, but is clearly crucial for virtually all projects, is the adequacy of the provisions made to ensure that the project continues to function when aid has been terminated. General issues of this type are increasingly covered in each aid agency by a formal manual of project appraisal, which all desk officers are supposed to observe.

Second, there are issues which are specific to particular sectors. Progress here has been less marked, but among several multilateral and bilateral agencies there has recently been a tendency to put increasing emphasis on the role of sector guidelines, which synthesize the lessons learnt from projects in that particular sector concerning the traps that lie in wait for the unwary, rather than on general manuals. This is a promising approach. Apart from the isolated horror stories, which seem to be distributed in a fairly random fashion across sectors and across regions, there are certain sectors or sub-sectors which are known among aid administrators as disaster areas. Rural water supply and integrated rural development projects immediately come to mind. Of special relevance for a discussion of technology is the fact that the record of aid agencies in industrial development seems to be particularly poor. Significantly, and usefully, the chapter on the findings of evaluation in a recent major study of aid effectiveness was cast almost exclusively in the form of a sector-by-sector analysis.[4]

Finally, there are what are known in the jargon of evaluation as 'cross-cutting' issues, which are of varying incidence among different sectors and in different regions. These are the hardest to handle. Because their incidence varies, it is difficult to build them into standard procedures. Because they are not specific to particular sectors (though there may well be sectors in which their significance is especially marked — for example, the impact on women in the context of African agricultural development), they cannot be fully covered through the medium of sector guidelines. Yet some sort of alarm system is needed. Two which are currently of concern are environmental impact and the impact on women. The choice of technology is clearly another such, though it is at present given perhaps rather less prominence than a few years ago. (This may well be a sign that the issue has indeed been effectively absorbed.)

Issues of general relevance to all projects were at the heart of the extended debate on the methodology of project appraisal which took place in the 1970s; and the early manuals reflected that methodological concern. The debate was conducted at a level of generality, however, which made it difficult to absorb into the day-to-day concerns of practical administration. The methodology of project appraisal, in itself conceptually quite simple, acquired a self-inflicted reputation for obscurity and complexity, haunted by seemingly arcane but in practice trivial issues, such as the choice of numéraire.

It has to be said that recovery was fast, perhaps too fast. Most aid agencies today rely in practice on simple check-lists, backed up in a growing number of cases by the discipline of some variant of logical framework analysis. The latter is no more than a schematic way of setting out one's objectives, the means to achieve those objectives, and performance indicators by which achievements can be measured. That seems simple and practical enough; and indeed aid agencies have a habit of emphasizing the simple and practical nature of their approach. But it becomes dangerous when it is used as more than a simple discipline, and becomes a crutch; and there is some evidence that this is what has happened.

Under the auspices of the DAC, the OECD Secretariat is at present undertaking a survey of aid agencies' approaches to project appraisal. The results should be available by mid-1987. Meanwhile, one can only offer some general observations to substantiate the charge laid in the preceding paragraph.

The weakness of check-lists, except in defined and repetitive tasks (and project design is far from being a defined and repetitive task), is that they tend to be open-ended. It is tempting to add in all the issues that might possibly arise. Now, since all issues cannot conceivably carry the same relative weight in all projects, the umbrella question has to be of the form 'Have you looked at. ... ?' For the harassed aid administrator, the instinctive response is to draw the two short lines involved in the making of a tick. In the case of general issues, and even to some extent sector-specific issues, he knows that the tick must have substance behind it if he is not to be at risk. In the case of cross-cutting issues, however, the tick may often and quite legitimately be vacuous. So a further element of judgement is required.

17

What, then, is the signal that tells the aid administrator that a tick is not enough? In the case of cross-cutting issues, the answer quite often is domestic politics. The three cross-cutting issues already cited — technology, environmental impact, and impact on women — clearly sprang to prominence partly from domestic concerns within the developed countries. There is an element of fashion in it, but behind the fashion there is usually substance. And certainly the results of these concerns, as applied to aid programmes, have led to significant new insights. One needs only to conjure the mass of significant empirical research on technologies for development that has taken place in the past decade in order to make the point.

Nevertheless, the political origins of such concerns have a continuing deleterious effect, not so much on the substance of debate as on the administrative response. The first response in most aid agencies is to appoint an adviser. In the nature of the appointment, the people attracted to it are likely to be evangelists.[5] They see their function, rightly, as being in part to heighten awareness of the issue in question. So they confront a dilemma. Do they seek to spread this awareness throughout their respective agencies, often battling against bureaucratic resistance, or do they consolidate their round with a small programme of labelled projects in which their role is unquestioned? At the political level, the answer to that question does not matter. The appointment of an adviser is itself the political response. At the operational level, however, the answer — or rather the balance struck between the two horns of this dilemma — is crucial.

The pressures all militate in favour of retreat into an enclave, while at the same time the evangelical spirit is reflected in frequent and implausible proclamations that the issue in question is universal. One of the characteristics of recognized cross-cutting issues is that they are usually upheld by an international network of small privately funded research institutes (ITDG and its sister institutions in other countries in the case of technology), which have a tendency to articulate their own received view. In the context of the work of the DAC, one is struck, when groups of specialist advisers come together from different agencies, by the participants' sense of relief when talking to their own kind, and their shared resentment over what they regard as inadequate attention to their concerns at the level of management in their respective aid agencies.

The substantive response is bound to be slow. In the DAC, the main instrument for fixing a substantive response to issues which have already been recognized in general debate is the system of aid reviews, whereby the Committee examines the aid policies and programmes of individual members on the basis of reporting guidelines prepared by the Secretariat. It is normal for the Secretariat to insert into its guidelines a few questions on major cross-cutting issues of current concern. An extensive survey of recent reports from DAC members reveals virtually no progress from the propensity to respond in such terms as 'Oh yes, of course, that issue is on our check-list for all projects'. So far as technology is concerned, as already mentioned, there is little evidence of further progress in key procedural areas such as procurement and the appointment of consultants, and recent trends point rather in the opposition direction of a reversion to stricter accountability.[6] At the same time, and in contrast, there has been a significant growth in the number of aid-financed projects which have an explicit element of technological innovation. So the problem is how to make progress from the now well-established narrow approach to a broader coverage.

The key to progress here is some sort of categorization as a basis for selectivity and for establishing an early warning system.

One may draw a useful analogy with recent work on environmental issues. At the end of 1982, the OECD's Environment Committee established an ad hoc group, under the chairmanship of Mr F. Evers (Netherlands), to examine the way in which aid agencies assessed the environmental impact of the activities that they financed. One of the first tasks undertaken by the Ad Hoc Group was to draw up a list of sectors or subsectors which were environmentally fragile. The early lists were highly selective and specific. The end-product was attached as an appendix to a Council recommendation adopted in June 1985, reproduced here as Annex I. In the intervening period, of course, the list had lengthened; and the list given in Annex I will probably strike most readers as too sweeping, especially when one looks at the lists of examples given in parentheses. But the general approach is clear.

Part of the trouble with cross-cutting issues such as the choice of technology is that it is in fact very difficult to find a parallel set of categories, sectorally or otherwise, which can be unequivocally ranked in terms of their sensitivity to technological choice. The empirical work has not been done. Most researchers in technological choice concentrate on particular fields, without any very clear intersectoral comparative framework; and at the anecdotal level the evangelical tendency is to seek examples over as wide a range as possible. If one were to try to construct a list analogous to the environmental list cited above, one might start, perhaps, with the following:

o Small-scale agriculture;
o Rural health;
o Rural roads;
o Small-scale industry.

But it is a safe bet that most readers of this paper who are specialists in technology will already have reacted with a feeling that such a list is much too short, and with some resentment against the tendency of non-specialist writers on the subject to box them in with labels such as 'rural' and 'small-scale'. And they are right. Indeed there is quite a different set of problems for aid agencies, noted by Robert Cassen in his recent study of aid effectiveness, connected with the transfer of high technology.[7]

What kind of empirical research is needed to support a more subtly differentiated approach? There is another analogy here, in the work of the DAC's Expert Group on Aid Evaluation. In 1986, the evaluation units of most DAC members' aid agencies co-operated in a programme which involved the incorporation of an agreed set of questions on one general issue and two cross-cutting issues in the terms of reference of virtually *all* ex-post evaluations undertaken during the year. The issues were:

o Sustainability;
o Environmental impact;
o Impact on women.

The list had to be selective, to avoid a long list of questions which would have ended up as a tail wagging the dog, diverting evaluations from their main purpose. The agreed questions are attached as Annex II. The results were due in mid-1987. There is a possibility that the choice of technology will then be included as an issue in a second round.

The purpose of the exercise was to establish the extent to which failure to take these cross-cutting issues into account in project appraisal and project design had had an adverse effect on project performance, and whether these failures could be categorized as being concentrated, in, for example, particular sectors or regions. Some evaluators would have preferred a case-study approach, the coverage of which would inevitably have been severely limited. It was an exercise that made some evaluators uneasy. Evaluators believe almost as an article of faith that the measurement of performance needs to be undertaken against some set of indicators established at the outset, whereas in this case they were being asked to measure performance in situations in which by definition no indicators existed. In the absence even of preliminary findings, one can do no more at this stage than take note of the exercise, as something to be followed up.

It should not be necessary in this paper to reiterate that the choice of technology is a complex issue, in which the factors to be taken into account cover a wider range than questions of engineering design in the light of relative costs. A reminder may be in order, however, to the effect that there is a strand in the literature on technology on the theme that in developing as in developed countries a preference for proven technologies is far from being so irrational as is sometimes claimed. The propensity for risk avoidance is something that the aid administrator needs to take into account — whether the risks to be avoided are those of project failure or trouble with his own superiors. The search for procedural devices to embed the choice of technology more firmly in the early stages of project design is in reality a search for signals to tell the aid administrator when a seeming strategy of risk avoidance is in fact a recipe for failure. To the extent that the search for more appropriate technologies is indeed a risky venture, it should be identified and funded as such by aid agencies, with an expectation of a high failure rate; but that is something which can be quite easily handled within the limits of what has here been characterized as the narrow approach, which is also the traditional approach, to technology as an element in the programming of bilateral and multilateral aid alike.

Annex I. Projects and programmes most in need of environmental assessment

Annex to a Recommendation of the Council of the OECD on Environmental Assessment of Development Assistance Projects and Programmes, adopted on 20 June 1985

1. Projects and programmes which are most in need of an environmental assessment can be identified on the basis of a number of criteria which aim at ascertaining whether the anticipated direct or indirect effects of a project or programme on the environment are likely to be significant.

2. When judging whether a specific project or programme may have a major effect on the environment, it is necessary to take into account, among other things, the ecological conditions in the area where it is planned to locate the project or programme. In-depth environmental assessment is always needed in certain very fragile environments (e.g., wetlands, mangrove swamps, coral reefs, tropical forests, semi-arid areas). When carrying out environmental assessment, issues which should be considered include effects on:

  (a) soils and soil conservation (erosion, salination, etc.);
  (b) areas subject to desertification;
  (c) tropical forests and vegetation cover;
  (d) water sources;
  (e) habitats of value to protection and conservation and/or sustainable use of fish and wildlife resources;
  (f) areas of unique interest (historical, archaeological, cultural, aesthetic, scientific);
  (g) areas of concentrations of population in industrial activities where further industrial development or urban expansion could create

significant environmental problems (especially regarding air and water quality);

(h) areas of particular social interest to specific vulnerable population groups (e.g., nomadic people or other people with traditional lifestyles).

3. Projects or programmes most in need of environmental assessment fall under the following headings:

(a) substantial changes in renewable resource use (e.g., conversion of land to agricultural production, to forestry or to pasture land, rural development, timber production);

(b) substantial changes in farming and fishing practices (e.g., introduction of new crops, large-scale mechanization); use of chemicals in agriculture (e.g., pesticides, fertilizers);

(c) exploitation of hydraulic resources (e.g., dams, irrigation and drainage projects, water and basin management, water supply);

(d) infrastructure (e.g., roads, bridges, airports, harbours, transmission lines, pipelines, railways);

(e) industrial activities (e.g., metallurgical plants, wood processing plants, chemical plants, power plants, cement plants, refinery and petrochemical plants, agro-industries);

(f) extractive industries (e.g., mining, quarrying, extraction of peat, oil and gas);

(g) waste management and disposal (e.g., sewerage systems and treatment plants, waste landfills, treatment plants for household waste and for hazardous waste).

4. The above list of projects or programmes is not in any order of importance and is not meant to imply that any particular project or programme type is necessarily more in need of environmental assessment than another. In addition, the list is not meant to be exhaustive as there may be projects or programmes not mentioned above which may still have significant effects on the environment in certain areas. Although the presence of a project or programme on the above list does not imply that such a project or programme will necessarily have significant adverse effects on the environment, and some indeed have positive environmental effects, experience has shown that there is often a need to take particular measures to eliminate or mitigate the adverse environmental consequences of such projects or programmes. Whether a project or programme should be subject to in-depth environmental assessment will therefore depend on an analysis of all the facts of the specific case.

Annex II. Development assistance committee expert group on aid evaluation incorporation of cross-cutting issues into members' 1986 evaluation programmes

Extract from a covering note by the Secretariat

The attached lists of questions were approved by the DAC Expert Group on Aid Evaluation at its meeting on 23-4 January 1986. The first and short list ('Terms of Reference') is intended for attachment to the terms of reference of evaluation studies commissioned by the participating agencies in 1986. The second and longer list ('Guidance for Evaluators') is to be retained by evaluation units as a basis for giving guidance to evaluators on the thinking which underlies the shorter list. Participants will be asked to synthesise the findings emerging from evaluations at the end of the year.

Incorporation of cross-cutting issues into members' 1986 evaluation programmes: Terms of reference

Most donor agencies who are members of the Development Assistance Committee (DAC) of the OECD have agreed to address the following issues in connection with their 1986 evaluation work. The outcome will be summarized at national and at DAC level in 1987 and used to improve the preparation of future projects.

The evaluation mission is requested to comment on *all* questions even in cases where the comment is merely 'Not applicable' or 'No time/data available to make an answer possible'.

1. *Sustainability*
1.1. What project benefits are likely to be sustained after donor funding ends?
1.2. What local capacities including maintenance systems (management, technical, financial, including provision for the replacement of capital equipment) are being developed to continue project benefits? Will they be in place once donor financing ends?
2. *Impact on women*
2.1. How were the interests and role of women taken into account at the design and appraisal stage? In what way did women participate in this process?
2.2. Were gender-specific data available or have they been developed since?
2.3. What are the effects, positive or negative, of the project concerning women's access to income, education and training, and with respect to workload, role in household and community, and health conditions?
2.4. Were significant factors concerning women overlooked at the appraisal stage?

3. *Impact on the environment*
   Note: The word 'environment' is taken here as referring only to ecological issues.
3.1. What environmental aspects were considered during appraisal?
3.2. If none, why?
3.3. What is the environmental impact, actual or potential, positive or negative, if any?

Note: Evaluators are invited to consult the Agency's central evaluation staff for further elaboration of the thinking which underlies these questions.

Incorporation of cross-cutting issues into members' 1986 evaluation programmes: Guidance for evaluators

The DAC Expert Group on Aid Evaluation has agreed on an experimental and voluntary basis to incorporate standard sets of questions on selected cross-cutting issues into the terms of reference of all relevant evaluations commissioned in 1986. The three issues selected are:

o sustainability;
o impact on women;
o impact on the ecological environment.

The questions that follow are intended as a basis for elaboration of the shorter list of questions which participating agencies have agreed to attach to the terms of reference of evaluation studies.

Sustainability
Project designs tend to assume that projects will be able to function effectively as donor support ends. The following questions are designed to examine and provide lessons learned as to whether sustainability will or will not be achieved.

(i)   What project benefits (or outputs) are (or were) to be sustained after donor funding ends?
(ii) What host country constituencies will benefit from project/programme success? How and to what extent has a constituency been built through project implementation? (Active beneficiary participation often helps to ensure the relevance and sustainability of development projects.)
(iii) What host country policies threaten sustainability of the activity? How are they being mitigated? What policies will support sustainability?
(iv) What organizational, institutional and financial capacities (such as management, technical expertise, cost recovery schemes,

e.g., user fees, staffing and incentive-structure and maintenance systems) are being developed to continue project benefits and to ensure adequate project administration? Will they be in place once donor financing ends? Will the organization have the capacity and flexibility to respond to changing conditions? What system has been developed to adopt (or adapt) new technologies?

(v) What financial provision is being made for operations and maintenance and the replacement of capital equipment, e.g., recurrent and capital costs?

(vi) Do projected benefits justify the continued investment of resources in the light of alternative opportunity costs and constraints?

(vii) What is an appropriate time period to ensure that the key conditions for sustainability will be created and operative?

(viii) What are the balance-of-payments implications of the project in terms of financing, continuing supply of spare parts and materials, and export promotion or import substitution? To what extent do these implications have a bearing on the project's sustainability?

Impact on women
(i) At the appraisal stage, what reasons were there for supposing that the impact on women should or should not be taken into account?

(ii) How were the interests of women taken into account at the design and appraisal stages? In what way did women participate in this process?

(iii) Were gender-specific data available or have they been developed during the project cycle, and how have they been used in terms of goal-setting, activities, resource-allocation, etc.?

(iv) What were the effects, positive or negative, of the project, concerning women's access to the following:

o production and markets;
o income;
o workload, division of work;
o role in household and community;
o health conditions;
o education and training.

(v) During project implementation or after project completion, did it appear that the impact on women differed from what was foreseen at the appraisal stage? In what ways? Does it appear that significant factors concerning women were overlooked at the appraisal stage?

25

(vi)   What was the impact of the inclusion/omission of consideration of the role of women at the design stage, and the participation/ non-participation of women in project implementation, on project performance?

(vii) What are the specific lessons for project design and implementation for future efforts in this field?

Impact on the environment

(i)   Projects with an explicit environmental purpose:

If the main project purpose is the achievement of an environmental benefit, then:

Were benefits as predicted?

If not, why not, and how was project implementation redirected in midstream?

If redirected, was a change made in the project strategy?

(ii)   Projects not explicitly addressed to environmental issues:

If environmental concerns were incidental to project design, then:

Was the project exempted from environmental review during the project approval process because it was thought that there would not be any significant negative impact?

Did significant negative impacts occur? What were these impacts and how were, or are, they dealt with during implementation?

If the project was thought to have significant negative impact and was analysed during project design as to the nature and extent of the predicted impact, was this impact mitigated or avoided?

(iii)   In both instances (i) and (ii) above what was the commitment and support of the host country to addressing environmental issues? How was this commitment manifest?

Is there a host country environmental policy? How did the project foster the development or implementation of such a policy?

Did the host country support the development of institutions for assessing environmental impact and environmental monitoring?

How were environmental issues and interventions incorporated into project management by both donor and host country?

How did the project involve host country environmental expertise in project management as a means of strengthening capabilities?

Appropriate Technology in the Norwegian development assistance programme

SVEN A. HOLMSEN

Deputy-Director-General, The Royal Norwegian Ministry of Development Co-operation

Introduction

THE QUESTION of applying Appropriate Technology to the difficult task of assisting developing countries is highly relevant for all of us who are engaged in this work. The general discussions on the issue in our Ministry have in particular been connected to the process of the transfer of technology. We have seen a tendency to focus on a one-way communication in the transfer process, where the importance of training and educating our co-operating partners has been dominant.

I feel that the message of this exhibition [ITDG's 'Design for Need'] with the focus on the need of the recipient — design for need — corresponds very well with the conclusions we have drawn during these discussions, and I hope that we, at least to a certain extent, have been able to act according to these conclusions in the implementation of our assistance.

The White Paper on development co-operation stresses the improvement of living standard and the creation of job opportunities as two of our main goals. We try to emphasize Appropriate Technology in this respect, for instance in giving priority to assistance which can relieve the work burden for women and by encouraging labour-intensive techniques which create job opportunities. When it comes to an analysis of our sector engagement in Appropriate Technology one will realize there are a wide range of technological levels, from the most advanced high tech in the telecommunications sector (considered as appropriate when applied in particular projects) to simple technology in for instance labour-intensive road constructions. Here I will give a few examples of this variety of technological levels applied in the Norwegian development programmes.

The question can of course be raised whether or not it is relevant to include 'high tech' in discussions on Appropriate Technology, but I have a feeling that the picture will not be complete without the high tech side. I will refer to four assistance sectors which are particularly relevant.

The telecommunications sector

If we first look at the telecommunications sector, our assistance has mainly been given to the countries in the SADCC region. These countries have defined their need for an inter-regional telecommunications system with the main political goal of achieving economic independence from South Africa. Such a system must be reliable, have an adequate capacity and be possible to operate and maintain for the countries concerned.

The choice of technology has been discussed intensively. The result of the discussions is that the same generation of digital transmission technology as is used in the Nordic countries is now being installed in Malawi, Mozambique, Tanzania and Zimbabwe. The advanced technology is made appropriate by assisting the telecommunication administrations of the countries in the technology transfer process with an extensive training programme, and a long-term engagement in technical assistance.

To a certain extent what is said about telecommunications also applies to the commercial energy sector, although the choice of technology here is more complex. An important guideline, however, will be to apply a technology according to the availability of spare parts and technical assistance. And there is of course the element of the professional standard and professional pride at the recipient end, making the choice of intermediate technology difficult.

The agricultural sector
Appropriate Technology within the agricultural sector is not a new phenomenon. People have dried maize in the sun, watered their shambas by the force of gravity, and made ox-ploughs and ox-wagons out of local materials, for ages. From experience we have learned that high technology projects are not likely to benefit our target groups — small-scale farmers, subsistence farmers, and women.

The introduction of more advanced technology has often increased social and economic differences. More land cultivated and higher production has in most cases meant higher income only for those few who are able to make use of the new technology, while the poorest subsistence farmers fall further behind, with lower income, less time for food crops and less time for the care of children. In such cases advanced technology has increased the social and economic differences, and can hardly be described as appropriate to the majority of the population.

To benefit this majority, local knowledge and the participation of the people must be the basis for the introduction of an appropriate technology. This technology can be an important factor for lightening the workload of women, particularly, whether the technology is directly connected to agriculture work, as with improved hoes, ox-ploughs, ox-wagons, maize mills, means of food processing (e.g. drying boxes); or when it is connected to daily household work as with a well with a hand pump near the village, or fuel-saving ovens.

28

The road sector
The scope for the promotion and development of labour-intensive methods of construction and maintenance of roads, is closely related to the following scenario describing a typical Ministry in a sub-Saharan country:

o the concerned Ministry's recurrent budget is limited, and is unlikely to increase in the near future.
o equipment operates about one-third of the time, and endless delays are encountered in procuring spare parts.
o political interference is unavoidable and results in continual requests for the diversion of maintenance equipment for non-maintenance activities.
o the large permanent work force is subject to civil service regulations affecting the hiring and firing of staff as well as incentive systems.
o the work force is poorly motivated and weakly supervised at the supervisory and engineering levels.

NORAD has, since the early 1970s, been one of the major contributors to the development of construction methods for labour-intensive road construction. The general development effort has mainly been channelled through the World Bank and ILO. The Bank has through a recently published report given a comprehensive overview of its involvement within the field of labour-intensive road construction since 1971, when the SOL programme was launched. (SOL stands for 'The Study of the substitution of labour and equipment in civil construction'). As stated in the report the programme was supposed to be 'a framework for research on and demonstration of construction methods appropriate for the socio-economic environment of labour-abundant and capital-scarce countries'. A group of industrial countries — Canada, Denmark, Finland, Germany, UK, United States, Japan, Norway and Sweden joined the Bank in establishing a Trust Fund to support the programme. Some of these countries have also been major donors for various labour-intensive road construction programmes.

The Bank's conclusion is that the application of labour-intensive techniques should merit close attention for civil works in about 50 countries where rural wages are the equivalent of less than US$4 per day. The Bank further concludes that developing countries will continue to need external funding for many years to come to establish labour-intensive work programmes. Likewise, it will be necessary to provide technical expertise. The final conclusion of the report states 'this project has generated an impressive multiplier effect in the awareness of people in developing as in industrial countries, that labour-intensive work methods offer a viable alternative, under certain conditions, to

29

conventional, equipment-intensive techniques and often provide a more efficient use of domestic resources.'

In addition to the World Bank, the ILO has through its Construction Technology Programme (CTP), been the major force behind the development of the technical concept. The basic idea of the CTP has been to develop methods which are technically feasible and competitive with equipment-intensive methods.

The major demonstration project which has successfully implemented labour-intensive road construction techniques, is the Rural Access Roads Programme in Kenya, where since the start in 1974 about 8,000km of gravel roads have been constructed. NORAD financed the Technology Unit which in the early stage of the programme was responsible for development of the construction methods. Since 1978 NORAD also financed part of the construction programme, covering about 1,200km.

In addition to the Kenyan programme, NORAD is at the moment involved in labour-intensive road construction and maintenance programmes in Botswana, Tanzania and Zambia. The main focus so far has been on the construction of low-volume feeder and access roads. There is however potential for further development of appropriate techniques of road construction. The next step will be to move into the minor and secondary road network with higher traffic volumes and higher geometric standards. This is the case in Kenya where the newly started Minor Roads Programme, for which NORAD is one of the major donors, comprises both improvement and maintenance of the lower strata of the classified road network.

One important aspect of the transition from equipment-intensive to labour-intensive road construction and maintenance is the employment generation, particularly among the rural poor. The job opportunities will both give direct employment and create indirect employment.

Another aspect is income distribution. It appears fairly obvious that the employment opportunities created by labour-intensive road construction programmes attracts the poorer strata of the rural population. The impact study of the Rural Access Roads Programme in Kenya ('Assessment of the socio-economic impacts of the Kenya Rural Access Roads Programme', Part I, MOTC, Kenya, June 1984) showed that a large part of the unemployed attracted to the road construction work were from the lower social and economic segment of the population. Forty-six per cent of the casual workers owned no land at all, and very little livestock.

The Kenya programme also gave employment opportunities to women, as about 15 to 20 per cent of the total work force was female. The report stated; 'those women who work in the RARP are typically disadvantaged in social and economic terms. Many seem to come from broken families, have their children when unmarried and have less education than their male counterparts.'

30

One of the major challenges for the developing countries during the next decade is to create job opportunities for the large and increasing number of jobless. The concept of utilizing labour-intensive methods in civil works, both in construction and maintenance operations should therefore be pursued both by donor agencies and developing countries. The total cost of establishing one job within the road sector is extremely favourable compared to the traditional industrial sector. The estimate from the Minor Roads Programme in Kenya is in the order of US$600 per man-year which is only a fraction of the cost of establishing a job in the industrial sector.

The water supply and sanitation sector
Probably no other sector can provide so many examples of inappropriate technology as the water and sanitation sector. The inappropriateness has been economic, social, institutional and purely technical in nature; the problems have been experienced by NORAD as well as other donors in their sector programmes.

Technology development and research undertaken as part of promotional activities under the International Drinking Water Supply and Sanitation Decade have played a major role in the changing attitudes towards technology selection. This is reflected in recent strategy documents prepared by NORAD to guide sector programme proposals for Kenya and Zimbabwe. The following aspects are considered:

o Utilization of water sources which can be developed with substantial local input,
o maximum use of local preferences, skills and economic resources with a view to ensure acceptance and sustainability;
o willingness by recipient governments to disregard traditionally accepted technologies, which are inappropriate in terms of costs or skills requirements;
o development of plans for introducing appropriate technologies, including training and motivation at all levels, local manufacture, revision of standardized technical specifications and general improvement of the local basis for water supply and sanitation technologies.

These items reflect clearly two of the predominant features of water supply and sanitation in developing countries: the interfacing of technology with social requirements and conditions; and the failure to provide services at an affordable cost.

A few examples of how Appropriate Technology has been applied within NORAD-supported programmes may illustrate the diversity of the problems.

31

Minor Urban Water Supply Programme, Kenya
Applied research for development and introduction of Appropriate Technology is supported. Important research has been conducted on alternatives to water-borne sewerage. The main subject has been to develop an appropriate technology for water-borne on-site disposal, and to gain experience with the introduction, promotion and maintenance of various low-cost options.

Pilot projects aimed at extending water supply services to low-income groups have been started. The objective is to find means of forming consumer groups which can take responsibility for managing communal water points on a co-operative basis. Access to the community water supply can be facilitated at an *affordable cost*, making the target groups independent of water vendors and/or polluted local water sources.

Borehole Drilling Programme, Zimbabwe
The drilling and equipping of boreholes began as a drought relief 'crash' programme. In the prevailing critical situation little consideration was given initially to the pre-requisite community involvement component. A task force was, however, set up to support the organization of local consumer committees, provide caretaker training and assist health education campaigns. As the strain of the drought eased, this community development component was gradually strengthened. This community development effort is required to improve the appropriateness of the technology in terms of acceptability, local skills, reliability and maintenance costs.

Rukwa and Kigoma Rural Water Supply Programme, Tanzania
The pumping of water from surface sources is inevitable for many villages within the project area. Hydraulic ram pumps have been introduced on schemes where excess water and sufficient head are available. The prime objective is to utilize an appropriate energy source and to avoid the diesel supply problem. These hydram schemes have been developed with a community participation strategy where maintenance training has been an essential element. In particular the long head-race channel is vulnerable to damage by flood, grazing animals, etc. Operational experience has proved the reliability of the hydram pump itself, but the civil structures have been more maintenance intensive than expected.

The fisheries sector
The path of the so-called 'transfer of technology' to the Third-World fisheries (and, for that matter, to many other branches of the economy) is far from being paved with success. In the past, too many fisheries development projects have resulted in fleets of laid-up fishing vessels,

heaps of rusted machinery, and decaying equipment. On the other hand, there have been cases where the introduction of technology succeeded all too well, and after a brief period of increased earnings, caused the further impoverishment of many of the fishermen, either because of excessive pressure on the available fish resource, or through inequitable distribution of the new technology.

The experience from Norwegian bilateral projects is two-fold: there are failures as well as successes. Assistance to developing fisheries in Tanzania from the beginning of the 1970s has not been altogether successful. Without going into too much detail, only some of the infrastructural set-up and education programme of the Mbegani Fisheries Development Centre relates to the needs of the major part of the sector, that is the small-scale fisheries. Briefly the technological gap is too great, as is the economic difference. The support of fisheries in Lake Turkana in Kenya during the late 1970s, by building a huge cold store, shows again that the mistakes over choice of technology re-occur, even for development support which is based on principles of untied aid.

This is because 'Untied aid' means not only untying from economic interests but also from our own technological and cultural background. What is transferred is consequently the 'knowledge of principles of technical relations which might be helpful for local innovation of new technological solutions'. Norwegian experts have a lot to learn in this respect. A certain humility towards local knowledge, local technical solutions and social relations carrying these patterns is essential.

Appropriate Technology means appropriate to local knowledge, habits and experience, to the household economy of each fishing family, to the local economic as well as social structure, and to the national economy. In relation to the latter, the consequences for the balance of payments of introducing different types of technology need to be borne in mind. For the fisheries sector we also have to add at least one more parameter and that is the resource aspect. The existence of a common resource which has limits is a constraint specific to fisheries. The existing resource situation is an important environmental consideration which is often neglected. To sustain the environment is an integrated objective of most fisheries projects, and technological solutions have to respect this.

In many Third World societies it is found that the successful transfer of a new and somewhat unfamiliar technology carries with it a great need for additional and complementary activities, such as guidance, extension and close follow-up, credit systems on easy terms, adult education. This is especially so under circumstances where the new technology involves the fisherfolk in individually greater risks, economically as well as socially. In realizing these needs, development projects have been re-designed in order to meet the need for this inter-disciplinary security net.

In many cases, however, it is found that countries do not have the capacity to take over projects involving a heavily subsidized security net. We experience that both in the long and the short run the organizational as well as economic feasibility of even such projects has to be questioned.

For a poverty-stricken target group even the above project set-up might be of great disservice because of the risks involved, together with problems of acquiring the knowledge needed for running the new technology. Withdrawal from the project would often be a rational action by the fisherfolk, resulting again in laid-up vessels, and motors rotting and rusting along the shore.

The question of Appropriate Technology in fisheries thus has to be answered in a holistic manner, taking account of the risk involved for the individual, and the background of the target group in a broad sense. Many projects have deviated from their target groups for these reasons. But the criterion that a technology should not *increase* the risk and uncertainty involved in earning a livelihood from fisheries for a target group is a strong criterion, which has to be considered all along the project cycle.

It is our experience that Appropriate Technology for the poor fisherfolk should generally be limited to improvements of the existing technology.

What technology is appropriate?
The fact that recipient countries actually request our technology, even if it is not suitable to their needs, has been and is a problem to be overcome, and is also due to a belief in industrialization, which exceeds the actual possibilities. Our experience, however, is that if we use more time for planning locally in the country in question, and plan together with the actual *users* in addition to national counterparts, in other words with persons who know the local situation, we can more easily come to an agreement on technological inputs.

Very often one finds that the most appropriate technology is not available. The 'choice of technology' might therefore be a concept not based on reality. The range of available technology, from the very traditional canoes to trawlers, for instance, is not a picture of a smooth and gradual change as is normal when societies try to bridge their own technological gaps.

But however broad the range of available technologies is, one still has to question the feasibility of each technology on each occasion. And the questions that should be asked as to feasibility include:

o Will the technology benefit the target groups by:

  – providing employment and/or income-earning opportunities to women as well as men?

34

- providing a lower priced and/or better quality product or service relevant to their basic needs?
- reducing the risk and uncertainty involved in earning a livelihood?
o Will the technology make optimal use of local and accessible resources/raw materials and energy resources, and minimize the use of scarce resources, notably capital and foreign exchange?
o Are the operational and maintenance requirements of the technology within the capability of locally available technical skills? If not, does the project foster acquisition of the necessary skills?
o Does the technological problem appear to be solved in a number of areas or countries in such a way that a general solution can be replicated in these areas and be adopted without major modifications?
o Will the project enhance the local capability for technology development and problem solving, and/or increase local self-confidence to be more innovative with unfamiliar technologies?

To conclude in a simple manner after this series of questions, I want to state: what makes the technology appropriate is that people get what they need when they need it.

Ecology and Appropriate Technology

PAUL HOFSETH

*Deputy Director-General, The Royal Norwegian
Ministry of the Environment*

READING SOME of the literature on Appropriate Technology I wonder whether it is perhaps futile to ask whether it is environmentally beneficial, efficient, or indeed whether it works at all. Maybe Appropriate Technology is a word of praise, and not a useful concept with which to classify technology. If I were to find Appropriate Technology projects that have caused environmental damage, some could reasonably object that since they went wrong, they were not appropriate after all.

Appropriate Technology is by definition suitable and successful; if it fails this proves that it is not appropriate. It is adapted to the society where it is introduced, and consequently its technical characteristics must vary. There are no particular, unique physical characteristics that can be used to determine its 'appropriateness'. If a technically identical project works in one place but fails in another, then it is just not appropriate there.

This opportunity to define away its failures is a versatile device. It is a terminological stable-door which need never be shut. Any horse that might bolt ceases to be a horse the moment it leaves its successful and well-behaved siblings. Appropriate Technology becomes a term of praise and not much more. Let me instead examine how Appropriate Technology could be judged if we were to set less elastic criteria. I will begin by establishing an arm-lengths distance from the intuitive conviction among many of the environmentally concerned that anything made of local materials by simple tools and skills must be beneficial; anything biologically produced or recycled is good, while the fruits of science, like the various plastics, should be avoided.

A dozen simple improved carts on a hand-built road can be just as destructive an aid to logging a threatened forest as a truck. A layer of butyl-rubber under the gravel will ensure that the small-scale water reservoir keeps its water. It is not the materials alone which decide between environmental success and failure. Neither do links with tradition or high technology alone make or break a project.

But, some may object, single materials or techniques may not be of any great consequence, but these are part of a web of production, trade and inter-related ways of applying knowledge. Polythene presupposes oil wells, refineries, trucks, noise, pollution and wholesale environmental destruction. If a poor country wants an ox-cart with ball bearings and rubber wheels one must have tyre factories, steel mills and factories somewhere: build them in ox-cart country or be forever dependent on deliveries from other countries.

So how to avoid swallowing the hook with the bait? In the counter-culture of the late 1960s, the *Whole Earth Catalogue* recommended opting out to become self-sufficient. One could buy gadgets to make commune life easier, or follow advice on the second-hand use of technological cast-offs. The latter is a definite blind alley. There is no sustainable independence in using car generators for windmills if the low price and ready supply of these depends on the huge industries one wishes to get away from. You cannot both discard mainstream technology and carry on using its products.

Another way forward is by stimulating 'low-impact technology' in the course of renewing ordinary industry. This is done continuously and is stimulated by emission rules, grants and taxes. It leads to reduced environmental impacts for the process in question, but not necessarily to lower impacts from the industrialized system as a whole. There is as yet no attempt at optimizing across industries. Maybe we need a review of our own system of production to make it more appropriate.

I believe that the most interesting feature of Appropriate Technology in the longer term is that one is forced to evaluate products, techniques and organization as part of a system. The idea of choosing technology à la carte is mistaken. The choice is between menus with some options, not between single courses. Are there other menus than todays? Are they better for the environment?

A look backwards may give us a better view of our own time. We can find similarities with current Appropriate Technology in devices invented in past millennia. The interesting feature of Appropriate Technology is not, however, its simplicity or its links with tradition, it is that it represents a reasoned choice. Appropriate Technology coexists with other means of performing seemingly similar functions. Why is this element of choice important? In the tradition of European planning, charting a conscious choice of technology may well have been founded by mediaeval monks. The holy orders opted out of mainstream technology to create and protect a sustainable society with its own values and culture. When the Luddites attacked the spinning-jenny they expressed sweeping generalizations about the goodness of one technology over another. Unlike Appropriate Technology this type of protest has got rather a bad name. The criticism of technology then, however, was not just an attempt to change one factory, it was a defence of a way of living. In both examples I feel that the physical implements at issue are far less important than the cultural implications.

Before Schumacher, William Morris, Patrick Geddes, Ebenezer Howard and Lewis Mumford discussed technology to achieve cultural aims. Some of them even created small islands of slightly different societies. It is this perspective of development aims that I find important. This, rather than the technical details of the choice of technology in Appropriate Technology merits a more thorough examination. By choosing each component carefully as part of a future system, Appropriate Technology may gradually lead to an appropriate society. I will not discuss current, industrialized-world technology here, although I believe that we also need to examine both our aims and the means we choose to reach them. I will however point out that there are numerous reasons why we in our countries should aim for less destructive ways of satisfying our needs, not to speak of our pleasures.

How then do we know if Appropriate Technology furthers a sustainable, environmentally benign development? Let us risk stating the obvious by listing some measures of development. It is not enough to equate development with growth, or the size of the GNP. In a situation with rapid improvements in infant health, GNP per capita may fall, public health in general may fall, but GNP may well grow. In a country with a large non-commercial and black-market sector, the official GNP may have a very tenuous connection with total useful activity. Even if the GNP did include these factors, one would still need some estimate of the distribution of wealth and opportunity in order to judge if development is proceeding satisfactorily. The most useful measures would seem to be linked to the actual provision of basic needs to the poorest. In addition we must make sure that this is done in a way which secures the long-term ability to carry on providing the desired level of goods and services. It is in this context one must examine the environmental effects of technology. Sustainable development requires technology that can be sustained.

This is the task of development agencies as well as environment authorities: to ensure that the means chosen do not destroy the basis for sustainability. So instead of asking in general whether Appropriate Technology is beneficial, I would set out to make demands of any technology to be used and wait to declare it beneficial until I have seen the answers to questions such as:

o Does it improve the environment directly? If not —
o Does it displace more harmful technology?
o Does it use materials, skills or capital better than the alternative?

I would then go through case by case. Does the proposed technology have environmental advantages in the fields that most directly affect peoples welfare? Does it have advantages in fields that have the greatest impact on the environment? Useful examples can be found in this conference, and my impression is that most of the technologies presented are indeed environmentally beneficial. My check list would be to look for Appropriate Technology for

38

o Water supply: drinking, sanitation, agriculture, industry
o Food provision: production, storage, distribution
o Clothing: biological materials—textiles, skins, hides
o Housing/buildings: raw materials: wood, soil, minerals
o Energy: energy use, biofuel/wood, mechanical power/hydro
o Transportation and mobile power: transport needs, animal power
o Services: human health, veterinary medicine, schooling

I would also make sure that each project was thoroughly analysed and followed up to make sure that both the local community and we as donors can draw on the experience gained.

Environmental concerns in development assistance should not just lead to the modification or the abandonment of projects so as to prevent damage. At the moment there is a desperate need for projects that can rectify some of the damage already done.

We do need impact analysis and well-adapted technology, but we have an ever-greater need to protect what is left of genetic resources in the natural habitats of the world. That can only be done by leaving large areas relatively untouched and by putting an end to the over-exploitation of the species. We must stop desertification and soil erosion. We must avoid the risks of global climatic change. We must try to prevent acid rain and persistent poisons from limiting the production potential of the poor world. There is also the matter of human health in the booming cities of the poor.

There is an enormous potential for better technology here, but I am not sure that this is within the mainstream of present-day Appropriate Technology. In order to achieve a better future I would hope that we can establish three types of environmental development project:

o for all development projects: ensure that they do not damage nature
o initiate special projects to restore given areas, and prevent further damage
o integrate planning to achieve a more environmentally benign society

In the long run it will be the development aims and ambitions which will determine the results. Perhaps the special strength of the Appropriate Technology movement depends upon these aims. They should at least be discussed from time to time, otherwise one might as well leave the engineers with a limit to costs and environmental impact, and tell them to get on with it.

Gender, culture and Appropriate Technology: a conceptual framework

MARIT MELHUUS

Institute of Social Anthropology, University of Oslo

MY BASIC ASSUMPTIONS here are three:

(a) the problems of technology are problems of organization;
(b) the problem of gender is not a problem of women or of biology. Gender is a socio-cultural construction. Therefore it is first and foremost a social relation;
(c) the sexual division of labour is basic to social organization. Because work itself has two dimensions — practical and symbolic — working relations transmit (and potentially transform) a cultural order.

First; addressing technology, whether appropriate or inappropriate, in relation to culture and gender, implies a perception of technology as contextually determined. This point of departure necessarily deviates from a more general view that technology is neutral (at best) or natural (at worst). Technology is socially constructed, socially consumed and socially evaluated. In other words, technology is not outside social relations, but embedded in them. Paraphrasing Philip Herbst who has stated that 'the product of work is people' we can say, along the same lines, that the product of technology is people.[1] In so far as we perceive technology as instruments of labour — and even managerial skills, expertise and know-how can be classified as such — technology is a part of labour, and labour is a form of organized activity (though not all organized activities are necessarily labour). Thus technology has to do with work organization. Therefore in discussing technology we are not discussing machines or materials but how material activities are organized. This brings us immediately to the questions of division of labour, the control over labour inputs and outputs, and the participation and decision-making in the labour process which in turn raises the issue of the sexual division of labour pertinent to my further argument.

Secondly let me at the outset make one thing clear: when I speak of gender I mean men and women. There seems to be a general attitude that gender is something women possess, whereas men are men. Gender is not a property peculiar to women. There are two genders, male and female, and they are structured in relation to each other. Gender is not

40

reducible to biology or sex. On the contrary, gender is socially constructed in the processes of socialization and the formation of social persons. Furthermore, the relative position of men and women is not based on equality. Gender is hierarchically structured and the place of women is on the lower rung throughout most parts of the world.[2] In other words, gender is a social relation, it is not a private or personal matter, and intrinsic to this relation is power.

Thirdly, the sexual division of labour is a basic principle of social organization. The sexual division of labour manifests one way of organizing work. There are of course many others (which I will not consider in this context). The sexual division of labour is reproduced through the concrete work of men and women. This division of labour is often perceived as a natural consequence of our biological differences. This is, however, in my opinion, a gross misconception, and I would rather state the issue in the following way. Work defined in its widest sense as both a practical and a symbolic field of action is a basic concept to our comprehension of the social categorization of gender. In other words, to paraphrase Herbst again: the product of work is gender.[3] Work reproduces a social relation. Through work one reproduces oneself, while at the same time reproducing others. Work and gender are fundamental elements in social organization. The organization of work reflects the organization of gender, and vice versa. Work and gender converge and emerge in the sexual division of labour.

This division of labour is manifest in many different aspects of social organization and is reflected in each individual's conception of reality, of 'self' and 'others' in ways we are only beginning to understand. Through the manifest expressions of work, who does what when, and its ideological justification, a cultural order is not only transmitted but also transformed.

Finally, as a consequence of the interlinking of these elements, I am suggesting that work tasks and work instruments i.e. both technology and know-how, seem to be gender typed. There is no escape from gender in this world, and to my knowledge there does not exist a gender-neutral work organization, either in the private or the public sphere.

To illustrate my points, I present for consideration the following cases: the effect of household technology on household organization in our Western cultures;[4] the impact of steel axes on aboriginal Australians;[5] and guinea pig production in the highlands of Ecuador.[6]

How many have seriously considered the paradox represented by the impact of technological innovation within the home on the homemakers of our Western cultures? The modern housewife of today has at her disposal a whole range of labour-saving devices (unthinkable in Norway some twenty years back). It is a technical revolution.

41

Hot-and-cold running water is taken for granted, as is electricity. Our cultural standard of living includes telephones, washing machines, vacuum cleaners, freezers and even automobiles as basic consumption items in every home. Some would also include dishwashers, sewing machines and food-processors as necessities for the running of a modern household. At the same time, the food and textile industries have taken over much of the processing which our mothers naturally included in their household chores. One could assume that housework would soon reach a point of becoming superfluous, or at least dramatically minimized, but the contrary seems to hold true.

The development of household technology both within and outside the home has made possible a considerable reduction in both work-load and work-time for household chores. It seems, however, that house-wives i.e. those not engaged in wage labour, are still occupied full time with housework and furthermore, that time spent on housework today is about the same as the amount our grandmothers spent. And this is in spite of the availability of household technology and a reduction in the number of children.

The household, whether a unit of production and consumption or just a unit of consumption, is an organization, even a work organization. Tasks have to be carried out and these in turn imply work and decisions about who is to do what. In other words a division of labour within the household is required.

It is usual to consider women's work in the house as a natural comple-ment to men's work outside the home. She keeps home while he keeps a job. This is a form of work complementarity that many will defend. Let us do so too, for the sake of argument. However, when the wife takes a full-time job outside the home this complementarity is displaced, yet women continue to have the main, if not the sole, responsibility for house and children. This means they are burdened twice, with a double work-load. This is a peculiar arrangement. Employment for women reduces the number of hours spent on housework (compared to the homemaker). But, employment for women does not change the basic division of labour. In Norway, for example, married men did only 10% of housework carried out, irrespective of whether the wives were working or not.[7]

It seems that households in our Western cultures are rather 'back-ward' forms of work organization, at least if we compare them with other types of work organizations subject to similar changes. Neither the introduction of new technology nor the radical reduction in the daily available manpower (sic) as a result of housewives going out to work seems to have any fundamental effect on the organization of the house-hold — if, that is, we do not consider women's overtime work as a fundamental change! In other words, the technological development has

42

not to any marked degree evolved a more flexible work organization on the basis of overlapping competence between men and women. Nor has women's employment changed the basic (complementary!) division of labour. And if time used on a task is a measure of efficiency, it seems that efficiency within households is declining despite the overwhelming presence of modern technology.

Without going into the details of household organization, it is important to note that households are organizations that run according to other principles than, for example, a factory or business enterprise. Its underlying rationality is different. The 'return' of household work is not money, but people; the product is not goods, but a home. The business enterprise has profit as a goal, measured in surplus of money (or capital) related to investments, where efficiency is a means to reach this goal. The household goal is its members' well-being, and in this perspective economic resources are means to achieve this overall end, and not an end in themselves.

The point I want to stress is that there is no necessary link between technology and work organization and efficiency. Technology does not automatically yield a certain type of organization with a specific rationality. More than anything, technology represents a potential that can be realized in very different ways according to the type of organization it is introduced to. In other words, the consequences of introducing new technology will depend on the organization's own rationality, that is, it's innate driving force, if you will, its basis for existence and its objectives.

I use this example from our own culture in order to illustrate a point which is very relevant when working in other cultures. Their rationality may be very different from ours and it is essential that we (1) recognize this possibility, (2) understand the basis for different rationalities when considering the introduction of Appropriate Technology.

Furthermore, the example illustrates very clearly the problems we have with changing some attitudes towards certain types of work, which are heavily gender typed, i.e. housework is woman's work. And finally, it serves to make visible certain aspects of the female labour situation which is rarely considered when we talk of technology and change.[8]

My next case is very different. It takes us back in time and across continents to a primitive group subsisting on fishing, hunting and gathering. The Yir Yoront is a group of aboriginal Australians who live at the mouth of the Coleman river on the west coast of Cape York peninsula. An American anthropologist who lived among them for 13 months from 1933 to 1935, describes the impact of the introduction of the steel axe (by the white missionaries) on this group (Sharp, 1952). A central item in their traditional cultural-technological repertoire was the stone axe. This axe was not merely a tool, but a symbol of masculinity and the relations of dominance. The stone axe was used in the production of other goods, and anyone — man, woman, or child — could *use* the axe. But only older men could *own* one.

It was primarily women who used the axe as it was their task to provide firewood to keep the camp fire burning all day, for cooking or other purposes... The axe was also used to make other tools or weapons and it was essential in the construction of wet season domed houses ... of platforms which provide dry storage, of shelters ... It was also used in hunting and fishing. In only two instances was the use of the stone axe strictly limited to men, for gathering wild honey ... and for making the secret paraphernalia for ceremonies.

The stone axe was also central in inter-group relationships, as the stone was obtained through trade with fixed trading partners outside their own group.

A woman or child in need of an axe had to get one from a man, and return it promptly after use. A woman would ask her husband, or, if he was absent, her older brother or her father. Only in extraordinary circumstances would she seek a stone axe from other male kin. A boy or girl would look to a father or older brother for an axe. All relationships where the axe was involved were ones of superiority/subordination. As Sharp says, 'the axe stood for an important theme of Yir Yoront culture: the superiority and rightful dominance of the male and the greater value of his concerns and of all things associated with him.' The axe represented the prevailing hierarchy of sex and age.

The shift from stone axes to steel axes provided no major technical difficulties. The new axes had few more or other uses, so that the practical effects were negligible. The work process per se was not affected, — but there were other consequences, unforeseen, which were rather drastic, upsetting the basic principle of work organization based on male dominance and authority through their monopoly of the axe. The white man believed that the steel axe was much more efficient, 'that its use would save time and that it therefore represented technical "progress" ...' The mission handed axes out randomly, as gifts or payment for services to anyone, irrespective of sex and age. Thus, the conditions for obtaining axes were no longer tied to long-lasting, pre-established trading partners, the obtaining of an axe was purely coincidental (seen from the local point of view). The numerical increase in axes caused a veritable inflation: axes were no longer a scarce resource. This, combined with the fact that they were distributed to younger men and women, created quite a different situation from the previous one where women and young men had to borrow axes and continually make visible their dependency on older men. The result was that the older men no longer had complete monopoly of all the axes in the bush community. To cite Sharp again: 'All this led to a revolutionary confusion of sex, age and kinship roles with a major gain in independence and loss of subordination on the part of those who now owned steel axes when they had previously been unable to possess stone axes.'

44

Sharp goes on to discuss the varying processes of disintegration of the traditional Yir Yoront society, relating it to their mythology and concept of time. He mentions the older men's desperate efforts to regain their power and prestige by establishing a new 'toothpaste' cult. The hope was that by substituting old materials for new ones in the magic cults these would become more potent. The malevolent magic was directed at the mission staff and some of the younger aboriginal men.

For our purposes, the example is illustrative as it shows very clearly how technology is embedded in social relations, and is even an explicit expression of them. The case also indicates the gender typing of certain tools (technology) and the effect on the society of 'trans-sexing' the tool, by transforming its 'gender property' in the process of making it available to all. In fact, the whole power structure of this society is undermined by the introduction in abundance without consideration of age, sex or status of the steel axe by the missionaries. The original content of the social relations are transformed and thereby the cultural order is also transformed; basically the relation between men and women, older and younger, and in the long run, the validity of their own ancestral beliefs and potency are questioned. A steel axe seems to be an innocent piece of technology to introduce to a society already in the habit of using a stone axe. It is merely a question of a substitution of something better, and a rather appropriate one at that. Yet, as is evident, it is not necessarily the size or the complexity of the technology which is introduced which is decisive for the degree of impact, but rather the *complexity of the organization* into which it is introduced — and in this respect it is knowledge of the workings of the society involved as well as the workings of our own thinking which is essential and which can be brought to bear on the results.

Lastly I shall turn to a project in the highlands of Ecuador.[9] The goal of the project was to modernize the peasant guinea pig production. The assumption was that there was a potential for increasing the production of guinea pigs. Marketing the produce was not seen as a problem, as guinea pigs are an important element in the local diet, and the demand was perceived as greater than the supply. Therefore the local population should be interested in a programme that aims at increasing the productivity and production of guinea pigs. Moreover, the project was directed towards women — a long-neglected target group for development implementation — as they were the main producers of guinea pigs.

Observations of the traditional way of breeding guinea pigs had made it evident to the experts involved (agronomists, veterinary experts and extension workers) that it was necessary to adapt a new package of Appropriate Technology to meet the project aims. The package consisted of the following elements:

o The breeding must occur separately and apart from the kitchen and living space of the peasants (where the guinea pigs traditionally were kept).
o Cages were to be designed and put to use in order to separate the guinea pigs according to age and sex.
o The breeding process was to be specifically controlled, to avoid inbreeding and weakening of stock.
o The feeding process had to be changed. The amount of feed had to be controlled in order to secure a better diet for the guinea pig. Alfalfa was considered the best fodder.
o By using cages, it was assumed that diseases could be identified more easily and controlled more effectively.

However, after three years of operation the project was not working: only twenty women had accepted the 'appropriate' package. It was then decided that an analysis of the cultural dimension was needed. The main hypothesis lying behind this decision, according to Archetti, was that something was wrong with the target population and not with the philosophy of the project and the teams. The mandate of the evaluation team of which Archetti was the leader was to find out why the Ecuadorian peasant preferred the traditional way of raising guinea pigs, in other words why they did not accept the new technological package.

Archetti's conclusion (to anticipate the discussion) 'is that the guinea pig is a key element in the articulation of a complex system of social relations within both domestic and public domains.' In other words, any change which impinges on the 'meaning' of the guinea pig involves a change in the 'meaning' of the cultural order. Briefly recapitulated, the situation is that guinea pigs are not just food. They are not just protein to be consumed anytime, anywhere. Guinea pigs are defined as extraordinary food — not ordinary food. They are used in ceremonies and at important events.

The transformation of food from extraordinary to ordinary (or daily) implies changes in a particular perception of that food's place in a social context. It would be like making caviar and champagne equal to hot dogs. The guinea pig is by definition a domestic animal. However it is also considered part of the household (even if it is eaten). This proximity of the animal to the household is related to qualities of the guinea pig, as a symbol. The Ecuadorian peasants also consider the guinea pig as an oracle. The 'utterances' and behaviour of the guinea pig are interpreted as signs of impending disease, visits, natural disasters etc. It is particularly the older ones which are endowed with this ability and therefore the strategy is to always have older animals in stock (not very conducive to productive breeding.) The guinea pig is used for healing purposes, but only animals *living with* (i.e. inside the home of) the sick

46

person can be used for the curing ceremony. Therefore the cages were not considered a viable alternative, because they moved the guinea pig outside.

Archetti argues convincingly that the guinea pig, and guinea pig consumption, was part of ritualized behaviour, and central to the transmission of particular cultural values. The guinea pig did not belong to the realm of commodities and cash, and only rarely were they sold. This in part explains the 'shortage' of guinea pigs at the local markets.

As mentioned, guinea pigs belong to the women and cannot be raised by men. At marriage one of the symbolic gifts that women receive is a pair of guinea pigs. When she dies her guinea pigs are slaughtered, after her burial, and eaten. The animals follow her destiny. Female identity, domesticity and guinea pigs go together. They belong to the same symbolic arena.

The Ecuadorian peasant women are overworked. Their daily chores consume more time than they have available, and therefore they have to make strict priorities in their allocation of time and labour. The technological package, appropriate for breeding better and more guinea pigs, implied more work for the women already burdened with household chores. The whole scientific approach to breeding, growing alfalfa, measuring the intake of food according to the size of the guinea pig, the selection of breeders according to a complex set of criteria, the periodical cleaning of the cages — all together increased the work load. Moreover, for the package to be successful these activities had to be done systematically because they were all integral parts of the new production system. In the traditional breeding system the tasks were fewer, and the production process itself much less time consuming. The raising of guinea pigs did not seem to conflict with the most urgent priorities of the women. Consequently, as Archetti explicitly states: 'To produce guinea pigs in the old way was not considered a problem. On the contrary, it is the new technology that presents a problem.'

The project assumed a want which was not felt by the target group; it also proposed a solution which created a problem. The aims of the project and the preferences of the people did not coincide. On the contrary, they appear to be quite contradictory. However, the tacit assumption in this as in many projects is that 'our' knowledge is better than, or even truer than, 'their' knowledge, therefore 'their' knowledge must give way to the new and true knowledge. Or even more blatant: their knowledge is not knowledge, but a bunch of irrational beliefs and therefore must (by force or by nature) yield to the only possible knowledge (that we know!). I think this position says more about our way of thinking, than it says about 'theirs' (whoever they may be). As an anthropologist I would suggest that we accept that there are different knowledges, and that all knowledge is relative. We must then recognize that there are different rationalities guiding action and decision making, and that these rationalities must be uncovered in order to be able to induce meaningful change.

I do not want to pursue here and now what I mean by meaningful change. Suffice it to say that as a primary criterion any steered change should be carried through with and on the premises of the people involved. Positive change will occur when the people themselves recognize that the alternatives presented are better than the ones they are familiar with. However, a pre-condition for even seeing alternative solutions is that a problem to be solved has been identified, *by the people who are to put into effect the solution.*

I hope that through these examples I have been able to present my case. I could have chosen another approach, e.g. listed all the negative effects of modernization on poor people in general and women in particular. However I am not convinced that an overwhelming documentation of how bad things are would be enough to change *our* attitudes, if we are not at the same time aware of how things are inter-related and how we, as products of our own culture, are programmed to think in specific ways. What I am saying is in effect, that this problem is as much — or even more — 'our' problem, as it is 'theirs.' Even though I concede that the problems are of a different order.

I have not talked about the situation of women in particular, though this must not be interpreted as yet another neglect about the plight of women. I hope to have made women visible through an explicit focussing on the gender relation and through a broadening of the concept of work to include that work which is not remunerated.[10]

I have also chosen not to discuss the problems of dependency, though I think that these are implicit in my argument. And finally I have said very little about technology and nothing about Appropriate Technology. This is not a coincidence. I am not an expert on technology as such. Furthermore, there is no clear-cut answer as to what Appropriate Technology is. As should be apparent, I would not necessarily advocate that small-scale, simple technology is more appropriate than complex technology. What I have done, however is sketch a framework within which the issue of Appropriate Technology can be perceived. I have argued that technology must be conceived within society and not without it. I have also tried, through concrete examples, to illustrate how technology works in very different settings.

Tools and knowledge are basic elements in any social formation. However, whereas in earlier societies (or other societies) tools were seen as a prolongation of man, it now seems that we see man as a prolongation of the machine. Techological development has not only implied an abundance of tools and machines for all kinds of purposes, it has also made possible a redefining and expansion of possible forms and objectives of production. But perhaps, and even more important, the technological development has brought in its wake a special consciousness about this development, a consciousness which reifies the process and puts it outside of humanity, where we somehow always seem to be lagging behind, and never seem to be able to catch up because the development is always ahead. And is not this powerlessness towards 'development' part of the same development? In my opinion, technological development is not primarily an expression of the existing technology — the advanced computer system or super-modern robot-run factories. Technological development will first and foremost say something about the relation between people and machines within different socio-economic systems. In other words, the use of technology cannot be reduced to a working manual or instruction booklet. The relation between technology and work, means and ends are culturally conditioned.

It is not the technology per se which is so interesting (I am sorry to say, as I know it facinates most of us) but *how* this technology is put into the system. Technology is part and parcel of our socio-material culture, it expresses part of our and others' history. Different technological solutions will represent different potentials not only for the design or implementation of different types of work operations but also for different types of work organizations. This is the essential aspect of technology.

One last point. I have argued that the sexual division of labour is deeply ingrained in cultural values. The work you do — or do *not* do — says a lot about who you are. In other words notions of work and notions of gender have to do with the construction of identities. And here we might run up against a problem, namely, that questions of identity are for psychologists and not for engineers, development planners and administrative personnel. However, I would contest that precisely because work and gender are so closely linked to identity and because development is primarily concerned with work, bettering work conditions through improved technology, increasing productivity through improved technology, and so on, this question of identity *cannot* be ignored.

Gender informs the pattern of learning, task allocation, hierarchy of leadership and decision-making, time-budgeting, etc. of most, if not all, work organizations (or perhaps any organization). In other words, work organizations are structured also by gender: tasks and things have gender – – new technology seems to be borne with it. These structures are often very difficult to see as they have the peculiarity of appearing to be natural. However, now that we are aware that this is 'going on' we should, by raising the issues and making the invisible visible, be one step closer to being able to do something about it. At least we can invalidate

49

the position that ignorance is bliss, and demand that these issues be taken into account. To pretend ignorance of basic working principles can no longer be an excuse for the unfortunate consequences of modernization through technological innovations or transfers.

The issue of Appropriate Technology begs two qustions: appropriate for whom, as well as inappropriate for whom?

A basic needs strategy: the ILO programme

IFTIKHAR AHMED*

Technology and Employment Branch, ILO

DESPITE SPURTS of growth in certain regions of the Third World, the overall poverty situation, particularly in rural areas, still remains acute. Even with an anti-poverty slant in its development programmes over the last two to three decades, Asian countries have yet to make a significant impact on mass (essentially rural) poverty. The number of poor in the Asian continent, especially the absolute poor, has been on the increase (ILO/ARTEP, 1986). No correlation is observed between the level and growth of incomes and basic needs' achievement in Africa, where the vast majority of the countries are caught in a severe economic crisis (Ghai, 1987).[1]

Under these circumstances, the technology programme in the ILO has had a clear anti-poverty thrust relying on employment generation as a major instrument for poverty alleviation. In consequence, the focus of these programmes has been almost exclusively on target groups at the grass roots level in rural areas where incidence of poverty is the greatest. It was also recognized that anti-poverty strategies cannot be successful if they do not effectively promote female employment and income, particularly in Asia where women's earnings constitute a significant proportion of poor households' total income (Ahmed, 1987). Similarly, programmes for reducing malnutrition in Africa cannot succeed without focusing on women's role in food production and processing.

The purpose of this paper is to review critically the contribution of the ILO technology programme to income generation and employment creation for specific target groups in different sectors of Third World countries. Account is also taken of the multi-disciplinary character of the problem and multi-sectoral approaches adopted for its solution.

With the above prologue, the paper begins with a review of the ILO technology programme in agriculture. It then focuses on forestry and concludes with an analysis of the rural non-farm activities where women workers predominate. The approach of the paper is to draw on the ILO

* Technology and Employment Branch, International Labour Office, Geneva. The views expressed in this paper do not necessarily reflect those of the organization to which the author belongs.

51

Table 1: Basic needs performance in Africa 1960–82[a]

	Life expectancy at birth (years)		Child death rate (aged 1–4)		Adult literacy (%)		Enrolment primary school (% age group)		Basic needs index[b]	
	1960	1982	1960	1982	1960	1985	1960	1981	1960	1982
Botswana	40	60	23	13	33	72	42	102	48	80
Lesotho	42	53	29	17	59	73	83	104	64	77
Gabon	36	49	34	22	12	62	100	202	54	72
Swaziland	38	54	33	27	29	68	58	110	48	74
Nigeria	39	50	50	20	15	42	36	98	35	68
Kenya	41	57	21	13	20	59	47	109	47	76
Congo	37	60	23	10	16	63	78	156	52	78
Cameroon	37	53	28	16	19	56	65	107	48	73
Malawi	37	44	58	29	22	41	30	62	33	55
Côte d'Ivoire	37	47	40	23	5	43	46	76	37	61
Somalia	36	39	61	47	2	12	9	30	22	34
Zambia	40	51	38	20	47	76	42	96	48	76
Zaire	40	50	32	20	31	61	60	90	50	70
Sudan	39	47	40	23	13	20	25	52	34	49
Madagascar	37	48	45	23	34	68	52	100	45	73
Uganda	44	47	28	22	35	57	49	54	50	59
Ghana	40	55	27	15	30	53	38	69	45	66
Niger	37	45	45	27	1	14	5	23	25	39
Chad	35	44	60	37	6	25	17	35	25	42

[a]Source: World Bank 1984: *Toward sustained development in sub-Saharan Africa* (Washington D.C.), *UNESCO Yearbook* (for data on adult literacy).
[b] The index is a simple average of figures on four basic needs with maximum of 100 under school enrolment and deduction from 100 for child death rate.

experience and utilize insights obtained from operational projects to orient development co-operation programmes in technology towards more effectively combating widespread unemployment and mass poverty in the Third World. Obviously, this analysis would shed light on strategies to be adopted for making the North-South development co-operation more effective in alleviating poverty. However, a concrete proposal for South-South co-operation promoted through an inter-agency effort is also discussed. Since the paper aims at reviewing benefits of technology to specific target groups at the grass-roots level, it has a strong micro focus, although important macro policy considerations are not ignored.

Agriculture

A review (ILO/FAO, 1985) of the mechanical technology in use in the eastern and central southern African region revealed that small-scale and subsistence farming, which constitute the bulk of the region's agriculture, rely almost exclusively on multi-purpose traditional hand tools. Such tools are currently used for nearly all agricultural operations, limit both the area cultivated and productivity, and do little to ease the heavy, arduous and time-consuming tasks of farming.

It was also observed that animal-draught equipment other than ploughs is scarce and existing ploughs are often expensive, made of low quality steel, and have unnecessarily high weight and draught characteristics. The potential for a cheaper and lighter plough and a wide range of animal-drawn implements and hand-operated equipment exists particularly for three critical farm operations — tillage, planting (seeding) and weeding — which are important for increasing productivity and the area cultivated, timeliness of cultivation, making the work less arduous, and promoting fuller utilization of labour in the rural areas of the region. It was also noted that ox-mechanization, even with the existing plough, enables farmers to increase the cultivated area, labour productivity and total production compared with hand-tool mechanization.

It was felt that the role of mechanical power technology should be to complement rather than compete with ox-cultivation in much of the region. In the event of a choice, encouragement should be given to private tractor contractors, who operate much more efficiently than the government tractor hire services. Available evidence suggested that compared to tractor farms, use of animal-draught reduces farmers' cost of production and ensures higher return per unit of investment and requires less foreign exchange.

The agricultural extension services do not appear to be geared towards the dissemination of farm equipment technologies. Their capacities need to be strengthened through training and technical support. A lack of well-defined national agricultural mechanization policies and strategies is observed, although a government-led trend away from tractorization towards the use of animal draught for the small farmer is now occurring in some of the countries of the eastern and central southern African region.

The successful development and testing of a number of farm equipment innovations in some of the countries of the region have not been followed up by programmes for promoting their widespread use. The evidence is quite dramatic that an equipment innovation on its own is not likely to be adopted, particularly when purchasing power is very limited. Widespread adoption has occurred only where there has been a good rural supply system for appropriate implements. These findings strongly suggest that no amount of farm machinery R and D work will on its own lead to the development of dynamic patterns of agricultural growth, no matter how good the equipment. Commercialization of the prototypes of these items have not occurred, although important insights have been obtained from efforts to promote their local manufacture in some of the countries (notably Botswana and Kenya).

The purchasing power constraint is so binding that even the annual operating costs of scaled-down farm machinery, like the tillage devices Tinkabi and Snail, are several times the average annual farm incomes of the target group. Animal-drawn equipment innovation packages, together with high-yielding varieties of crops, are more likely to be adopted, since the cost of the equipment innovations are more than covered by the additional output generated in a single season (Ahmed and Kinsey, 1984).

It is found that the farm equipment manufacturing capacity is, in general, weak or non-existent and is constrained by lack of raw material (foreign exchange availability) and markets. It was concluded that local manufacturing should be geared through small-scale rural industries and repair facilities to finish, assemble and retail semi-finished products available from the factory-scale manufacturers. Rural blacksmiths need to be trained and their capacities and facilities upgraded.

Having noted the inefficiencies arising from marketing and distribution of farm equipment through public sector bodies, consideration could be given to alternatives, like greater reliance on the market mechanism.

It was observed that whereas R and D has been successful in generating and developing farm equipment technology in the public sector, there is a pronounced lack or non-existance of links involving organizational, financial and technical co-operation and co-ordination among government institutions, financial bodies, distribution channels, and commercial businesses, for getting the technology into the hands of the final users. Governments, recognizing the importance of this, are anxious to forge such links — as is evidenced by pilot experimental projects initiated locally in Botswana, Kenya and Ethiopia.

Forestry

Technologies appropriate for forestry would, ideally, improve working conditions, enhance the safety of work, protect the environment and generate a large volume of employment. Considerations of the quality of work are of particular concern to forestry workers, since theirs is one of the most strenuous and hazardous of occupations. Compared with other sectors, forestry has always suffered high accident frequency, severity and fatality rates in a wide range of countries.

An ILO project in the Philippines revealed that intermediate or improved labour-intensive technologies for Philippine forestry do exist (J. Laarman *et.al.*, 1981). Their use leads to increased productivity when compared with more primitive techniques, but decreased labour displacement when compared with more capital-intensive ones. In addition to generating productive employment, these intermediate technologies offer in varying degrees the advantages of improved working conditions, less risk of injury, and greater protection of the environment.

These conclusions relate to the basic forestry operations of felling and the cross-cutting of trees, thinning, log transport, log loading, underbrush clearing, tree planting and pruning. As an illustration, technological alternatives for two of these operations are discussed.

Three alternative methods of felling and cross-cutting trees of large diameter were examined. The first involved use of the large, heavy-weight power chain saw of 9 to 13 horsepower, equipped with a long guide-bar. This is the predominant method in the Philippines for large-diameter timber. It has replaced manual felling with the two-man cross-cut saw, which was the traditional method until the 1960s.

The project introduced a smaller and lighter power chain saw of 3 to 5 horse-power as the third and intermediate alternative. The small chain saw cut somewhat slower than the large chain saw, but three times faster than the two-man cross-cut saw. Hence, labour productivity and labour usage were balanced between the two extremes.

The lowest cost of $19 per 100 cubic metres (all costs are given in US dollars) was achieved by the intermediate method, the small chain saw, compared with $23 to $26 for the large chain saw, and $22 for the manual cross-cut saw.

Apart from direct monetary savings, the small chain saw has advantages in terms of health, safety and the environment. Manual sawing in tropical climates places great physical strain on the workers, especially if their diet is not completely adequate. The large chain saw is no better, since it is heavy and entails a high risk of accidents and hearing loss. In contrast, the small chain saw is equipped with anti-noise and anti-vibration devices; it is light and well balanced.

Three alternative methods of removing bark from pulpwood were compared. The capital-intensive method was mechanical debarking.

The most labour-intensive method was the use of the bolo.[2] The project introduced a properly designed debarking spud (a long-handled tool with a small spade-like head) as the improved manual alternative.

Use of the debarking spud in place of the bolo increased labour productivity by between 33 and 129 per cent, depending on timber species and bark characteristics. Yet the debarking spud absorbed considerably more labour than the mechanical debarker.

Ergonomic considerations played an important role in the difference between methods. When using bolos, the workers were constantly stooping; in contrast, the debarking spud allowed them to maintain a semi-upright stance. Use of the spud also reduced the risk that the workers would lacerate themselves, as frequently occurred with the bolo. Moreover, when used to debark pine, the spud helped to reduce bodily contact with the resinous wood.

The intermediate technologies are often the least-cost alternatives at prevailing market prices. This is very important if they are to receive serious consideration and acceptance by employers and other decision-makers in the forestry sector.

It is also important to recognize the implications for factor shares. The intermediate technologies direct a large share of factor payments to labour in the form of wages. The equipment-intensive technologies direct a large share of factor payments to capital in the form of machine costs.

The smallholder tree farmers involved in the agro-forestry practices of fast-growing tree species adopted many of the labour-intensive harvesting (e.g. water buffalo-drawn equipment, such as harnesses and log trailers) and planting tools in the Philippines. Some of the intermediate technologies, such as the farm tractor skidding winches, were adopted by the private sector commercial forestry concessionaries (ILO/BFD, 1982).

Women and rural non-farm activities
In the non-farm sector of the rural areas of Third World countries women are more likely than men to be unpaid family workers; to be casual labourers working seasonally rather than year-round; to be unemployed and looking for work. They also earn consistently lower wages, compared to the men, for the same tasks. Those women with gainful employment saw their purchasing power drastically eroded and this loss obviously could not be offset by increasing their number of days of employment. Compounding these gender-based differentials in monetary and declining real wage rates is the concentration of women into tasks marked by low productivity and low returns (the most undervalued and underpaid sectors of production). Under such circumstances the role of technology should be to raise women's labour productivity

(because this raises the returns to their labour), expand poor women's productive employment opportunities, reduce women's work burden and eliminate drudgery (Ahmed, 1987). The governments of most Third World countries have all proclaimed the integration of women in the development process to be a major goal.

Post-harvest processing. Of the 460 million days of rural employment in crop processing in Bangladesh, 80 per cent is generated by rice processing alone (Government of Bangladesh, p.108). Women's labour accounts for 86 per cent of this employment. Labour requirement for husking, which is entirely a woman's job, constitutes 52 per cent of the total post harvest employment (J.U. Ahmed, 1982). While post-harvest earnings as a proportion of total women's earning is nearly 40 per cent, women's earning from rice husking by traditional ('dhenki')[3] technology as a proportion of total post-harvest earnings is 60 per cent (Salahuddin, p.29) and constitutes a major source of livelihood for women from landless or near-landless households. The rapid growth of mechanized milling has led to the displacement of 3.5 to 5 million days of female labour per year (Bangladesh, p.108). There are now 11,000 rice mills in Bangladesh, most of which are electric or diesel engine-operated rice hullers, but about 50 are automatic or semi-automatic (Ahmed 1985, p.29). Jobs created by the new technology, though fewer in number, are almost exclusively male. This is a glaring example of a technological change which is not sex-neutral.

Capital/labour substitutions as a result of relative factor price distortions in environments of surplus labour are by now well known. Such distortions have led to a reduction in the price of capital below its equilibrium level (i.e. its marginal value product) while forcing the price of labour above its equilibrium. As a direct consequence entrepreneurs naturally tend to take advantage of the relatively cheap factor (capital) and economize on the relatively expensive one (labour). Although this simple economic principle is rigorously applied to any conomic activity irrespective of the sexual composition of the labour force, it still appears to constitute a very valid explanation for the displacement of female wage labour in, for example, rice processing in Asia, particularly Bangladesh and Indonesia.

In the rural areas of Bangladesh, government policy of extending rural electrification and credit to small-scale industries has made the net return (value added minus labour costs) per unit of capital 48 per cent for rice mills, when financial institutions charge less than 15 per cent per annum for credit provided (ILO, pp.62–3).[4] At the same time, while the return on labour when mills are used is 139 to 163 per cent higher than the wage rate, it is only 22–34 per cent higher when the traditional dhenki technology is used.

57

That the incidence of unemployment resulting from this technology is overwhelmingly on the women from landless households in the labour market is revealed by the fact that the vast majority (73 per cent) of the mill owners had previously hired female wage labour for rice processing (Begum, 1985, p.238). The reduced labour use is now entirely male. With the adoption of the new technology, women from wealthier households do not have to supervise hired female labour. For those peasant households which have the cash for milling, the unpaid female family helps are relieved from the time-consuming and physically demanding task.

The calamity of women's job losses from similar technological change is by no means smaller in neighbouring India. There too the milling technology was adopted for economic reasons (relatively lower cost of processing) and it is estimated that 125 million women days of work per year have been lost, representing an income for women from poor households of about US$55 million. The fact that with technological change, the men (though in fewer numbers) usurped these jobs is revealed by the fact that the corresponding annual gain in male wages in rice milling was of the order of US$5 million (Srivastava, 1985, p.407).

Outside the South Asian sub-continent, in Indonesia, mechanical rice hullers were well subsidized since credit was available for their purchase at an interest of one per cent per month, whereas regular village credit cost five to ten per cent per month (Cain, 1981, p.833). As a result, the cost of commercial milling was low because of the over-capacity of the many new mills set up in Java (Tinker, 1981, p.73). The consequences are by now well known. The estimated reduction in women's work days was 12 million, with a loss of $50 million in earnings. Ten per cent of these payments were in food, which meant a ration which served as four month's food consumption for the family was lost (Collier, 1974).

There have been other economic losses to the poor households from this technological change. Following hand-pounding, by-products like rice husks are used as fuel for parboiling rice, or are sold to potters for firing. Rice bran is fed to animals, poultry and fish. Given the momentum gained in the spread of the technology, it is clear that rice mills are now a *fait accompli*. There are three possible policy options:

(a) Provision of collateral-free loans to poor women displaced by the technology to own and operate the rural rice mills in groups. This has been accomplished with remarkable success in Bangladesh where the Grameen Bank has extended credit to groups (membership ranging from 30 to 40) of poor women, to purchase rice mills for business operation. The loan recovery rate achieved was 99 per cent, and the income of the borrowers went up by 26 per cent in two years (Ahmed 1986a, p.39). In 1984 alone, 70 collective enterprises

58

by women secured loans for rice hullers (Grameen Bank 1985, p.32). This success story could be replicated in South Asia.

(b) The development and introduction of intermediate technologies which raises women's productivity and reduces labour displacement could be another strategy. Indeed, in Bangladesh an intermediate technology prototype (improved dhenki) is currently available. The following comparative assessment emerges (Table 2): (i) unit milling cost is the lowest for the improved dhenki; (ii) there is no labour displacement following the use of the intermediate technology compared to the traditional method, while labour productivity is 11 times higher than the traditional one; (iii) while the capital cost is respectively 833 times, 36 times and 2.3 times higher for the automatic, rural and improved dhenki mills compared to the traditional dhenki, the corresponding productivity increases are 14, 23 (at current capacity utilization) and 11 times respectively.

Table 2: Alternative technologies in rice husking: Bangladesh, 1984[a]

Technology	Capital cost (takas)[b]	Rated hourly production (tonnes)	Employment (no. of persons)	Capital Intensity (capital cost per worker) (takas)	Milling cost (per tonne)	Labour productivity (value added per hour) at rated capacity	at 40 per cent (current) utilization
Automatic mill	8,000,000	2.030	30	266,666	163	180	72
Rural mill	70,000	0.750	6	11,666	171	291	116
Improved dhenki	1,800	0.060	2.5	720	58	54	—
Dhenki	800	0.006	2.5	320	585	5	—

[a] Source: Q.K. Ahmad and Rafiqul Islam, 1984.
[b] In May 1984 there were 26 takas to the US dollar.

Similarly in India an intermediate mini rice mill developed by the Central Food Technological Research Institute is capable of processing small quantities of paddy with the same efficiency, quality, and standard of large mills (Srivastava, 1985). This composite mill can carry out cleaning, shelling polishing and separation operations.

(c) For both the above options credit to cover fixed capital costs will have to be provided. Provision of training would be important, as skills are not only an important determinant of labour productivity but also will help prevent the job becoming a male job.

Vegetable oil extraction and cloth weaving. Technological dualism is observed in oil extraction (animal-powered vs engine-powered oil mills) and cloth weaving (handlooms vs powerlooms vs modern mills) in Bangladesh (Table 3). The fixed capital per worker in the modern technologies is 7.5 and 16 times higher compared to the traditional technologies in oil-seed crushing and weaving respectively. In contrast the labour productivity gains are only 5 times for weaving. As noted earlier in the cases of rice mills, incentive to adopt oil mills is high, as the net return per unit of capital is 72 per cent (ILO, 1985, pp.62–3). Its impact on employment is both quantitative and sexual. Female jobs are taken away by the males, but in fewer numbers. While over 30 per cent of the workers under *ghani* processing were women, no women at all were employed by the oil mills (Ahmad, 1986b, p.46).

Table 3: Alternative technologies in oil-seed crushing and cloth weaving: Bangladesh, 1980[a]

Processing technologies	Capital/labour ratio (Value of fixed-assets per worker in takas)	Output/capital ratio (Value added per taka of fixed assets in takas)	Output/labour ratio (Value added per worker in takas)
Oil-seed crushing			
Ghani[b]	2,882	2.22	3.74[c]
Oil mill	21,716	5.00	36.57[c]
Cloth weaving			
Handloom	1,583	2.81	4,461[d]
Power loom	26,061	0.87	22,673[d]

[a] Source: Ahmad 1986b, p.46 and 1986a, p.22
[b] Traditional animal-powered technology
[c] Value added per labour hour
[d] Annual value added

Bangladesh women's participation in handloom production is currently confined to reeling only and could be expanded to include weaving as well. That women of Bangladesh are active in the weaving industry is reflected by the fact that in 1984, nearly as many landless women (929) as men (1074) took Grameen Bank loans for weaving (Grameen Bank, 1985, pp.23–4).

Production linkages

In this section, an attempt is made to trace the impact of technological change in men's activities on women's employment and incomes through the operation of the production linkages and sex-sequential nature of the labour process. This is attempted in terms of three industries import-ant for South Asia (fish, dairy, and coir industries) in which both men

60

and women participate. In addition to tracing these linkage-related indirect impacts, an attempt will be made to assess the consequences for women's employment and incomes of technological change directly on those segments of the labour and production processes in which women are engaged.

The fishing industry. The primary emphasis of a fisheries development project in Kerala, India, was on the mechanization of fishing boats, the introduction of ice and improved freezing techniques for the preservation of fish, and the use of insulated vans in fish disposal. Traditionally, men were responsible for harvesting fish while women participated in its preservation, distribution and marketing. In designing the above project, little account was taken of this sexual division of labour (Gulati, 1984a).

The nature and character of technological change in the fishing industry are highlighted as follows: (a) where no mechanized boat was available before the project, over the years there has been a steady increase in the number of mechanized boats owned by fishermen and a decline in the number of traditional crafts (Table 4); (b) the use of ice for preservation has taken firm root and expanded uniformly. Even the women headload fish vendors use ice; and (c) there has been a significant growth in the infrastructure facilities in terms of the production of ice and the establishment of freezing and cold storage capacity (Table 5).

Table 4: **Backward linkages to boat and gear technology in fishing. Kerala: changes in mechanized boats and traditional crafts 1953–80[a]**

| Year | Mechanized boats | Traditional craft | |
		Thanguvallom (large plank-built craft)	*Kochuvallom* (small plank-built craft)
1953	–	197	280
1959	63	123	260
1963	87	93	135
1976	144	35	48
1980	419	40	147

[a] Source: Leela Gulati, 1984a, p.8

61

Table 5: Forward linkages from boat and gear technology in fishing. Kerala: growth in ice plants and fish freezing plants 1953–76[b]

| Year | Ice plants | | | Freezing plants | | |
	No.	Production (tonnes)	Storage (tonnes)	No.	Freezing capacity (tonnes)	Frozen storage capacity (tonnes)
1953	–	–	–	–	–	–
1963	1	25	200	1	9	125
1968	–	83	385	–	37	400
1976	29	377	325	15	88	1,625

[b] Source: Leela Gulati, 1984a, p.13

There was a phenomenal increase in the volume of the fish catch and the composition improved with a larger share of prawns, which boosted the export earnings from marine products.

Although the designing of the technology project was sex-blind, ex-post evaluation reveals positive socio-economic gains to both sexes through the operation of production linkages, as elaborated in Table 6.

For women, work opportunities have been stimulated upstream in net making and coir processing, and downstream in prawn processing, marketing and trade, both for wages and through self-employment. Similar increases in employment and incomes were noted from the phenomenal increase in the number of ice plants, and in freezing capacity (Table 5). Women not only gained economically in quantitative terms, their work participation improved qualitatively. Before the technological change, women from socially disadvantaged households (widowed, divorced, aged women, and unmarried girls from single parent households) accepted paid work. Now, married women and unmarried girls from two-parent households account for the large majority of working women (Gulati 1984a, pp.61–2).

However, the significant unanticipated positive socio-economic gains made by women are threatened by developments affecting their new income opportunities directly: (a) the introduction of nylon nets, fabricated by machines (and which also facilitate a larger catch) produced in factories being encouraged by the government is threatening women's livelihood (Gulati 1984b, p.2094) and (b) the introduction of an auction system of marketing has forced women to compete with large traders, causing them to lose out in their livelihood from fish marketing

62

Table 6: Women's employment generated through production linkages to boat and gear technology in fishing: Kerala 1978 (percentage of working women from fishing households)[a]

Type of linkage and activity	Village		
	Sakthi-kulangara	Neenda-kara	Puthen-thura
Backward linkages			
Net maker	4.0	6.5	68.9
Coir processing for fibring	2.0	0.5	2.1
Forward linkages			
Prawn processor for wages	26.3	23.0	24.0
Prawn dealer	44.5	35.9	0.5
Prawn dealer at home	2.0	8.8	0.1
Fish business	–	–	0.5
Shell collector	–	4.6	–
Fish headload vendor	17.2	7.8	0.6
Others	4.0	7.4	3.3
Permanent employment	–	5.5	–
Total	100.0	100.0	100.0

[a] Source: Leela Gulati, 1984a, p.39

(Ibid., p.2023). From a policy point of view, clearly women's jobs need protection in the case of (a) above. Provision of risk capital (free of collateral requirements as in the case of Grameen Bank in Bangladesh) could provide some support to women against the financial muscle of speculative wholesale bidders at the fish auction market.

The dairy industry.[5] Two alternative technologies for milk preservation were in use in Pakistan Punjab. The most common method of preserving milk during transportation is by putting ice in the cans of milk. This not only dilutes the milk, but also contaminates it when the ice is made from impure water. On the other extreme a sophisticated and costly sterilization process involving steam injection and packaging tetrahedral containers, was planned for Okara, Khanewal and Rahim Yar Khan. A third alternative installed at the Shah Jewna Livestock Farm in Jhang District in the Punjab is a locally manufactured sterilizer facility which uses domestically made equipment and materials which are simple to use and maintain, e.g. sterilizer, gas cylinders, burners and bottles, and on which an internal rate of return in excess of 30 per cent could be earned.

This intermediate milk preservation technology has strengthened the backward production linkage with villages surrounding the plant. The marketing and production of milk thus stimulated will benefit women responsible for feeding, tending and milking in peasant-proprietor families, and among tenant and landless families (S. Abida Hussain and Faizia Aziz, 1981, pp.68–9). Backward linkages to the domestic capital goods industry would bring benefits to the male population as well. Given the enhanced shelf life of milk, the marketing of the bottled milk is not a constraint and generates employment in the service sector.

Although the women do most of the work in producing the milk and clarified butter (*ghee*), both of which fetch substantial profit, the earnings are pocketed by the man of the family. In response to this situation, the Women's Milk Collection Association of Shah Jewna has been organized, to give women an opportunity to earn an independant income.

The introduction of a dairy scheme in Andhra Pradesh, India, under state auspices essentially meant the collection of milk from a large network of milk centres in villages, the chilling in milk plants located in small towns, and the marketing in urban areas. Through the backward linkages it increased the work load of women from marginal peasant and agricultural labourer households, and the cash earnings generated by the women's activity are grabbed by the males. Credit facilities for the purchase of animals were extended to the men despite this being women's responsibility (Mies 1986, pp.80–82). Similarly, improved veterinary advice went to the males of Gujarat even where women were responsible for the animals (ESCAP 1981, p.20).

The coir industry.[6] Women's work in the coconut/coir industry of Sri Lanka has traditionally been that of processing rope. Coir production also represents a sex-sequential labour process. Males are exclusively responsible for dehusking, transportation by car, making and cleaning husk pits. Filling husk pits are shared by males and females. Females are exclusively responsible for emptying husk pits, hammering soaked husks, drying fibre, cleaning fibre, spinning rope by hand, and transport on foot. Whenever spinning involves superior quality work by hand or spinning rope by machine, or is done in an ergonomically superior posture, men participate.

From this sexual division of labour, it is clear that the most demeaning and degrading task of emptying husks from pits is assigned to women. Typically, women remove husks during several hours in breast-deep water in the stench of the fermentation process. The women (usually the

64

poorest in the village) also remove the stones and logs covering the pits: they also have the heavy task of hammering the soaked husk with a small wooden club, until the fibre is loosened (20 to 30 blows for a well-soaked husk). Wooden 'fibre-cleaning' machines are available on rental from traders. Organizational and financial support need to be extended to women who cannot afford it. In contrast, land expansion and the emphasis on cash crop production in Africa has led to the greater expropriation of the unpaid female family labour input for planting, weeding and harvesting (I. Ahmed, 1985).

Factor market imperfections
The existence of a high degree of factor market imperfection in the rural areas of most developing countries is fairly well documented by now. The main feature of this imperfection is that access to factors of production is much easier for some groups than for others. (I. Ahmed 1985). Even in the absence of technological change, the existence of such a phenomenon affects the allocation of resources, the methods of production and the distribution of rural incomes. With technological change, when there is a greater need for credit, modern means of production, knowledge of new technology, extension services, participation in rural organizations, etc., the question of the access of disadvantaged groups to these factors is of crucial significance.

Consequences for women. Analysis with respect to rural factor market imperfections has almost always been focused on class-based inequalities. It has nevertheless been convincingly established that inequalities may be sex-based as well, in that rural women are systematically denied access to land rights (and hence as in Nepal to collateral for loans), tenancy, resources, training, farm inputs, extension services, and modern means of production. Furthermore, there are biases among male extension agents who regard women as deserving of advice only in the area of home economics. Such discrimination is due not only to an ignorance of women's roles but also to the fact that the household is treated as the unit of production with all services being chanelled through the male head.

Sex-based discrimination is most glaring in cases where women engaged in farming and livestock are ignored by extension agencies, despite the fact that in some countries of Asia (e.g. Nepal) and Africa, such as Botswana, Tanzania and Kenya (Carr, 1985), women farmers are as efficient and progressive as their male counterparts, even though they do not enjoy the same advantages. This efficiency may be due to more intensive use of female family labour and, as observed, due to more progressive farm management. Just as high labour intensity on small farms is a manifestation of the existence of rural factor

65

imperfections, rural women's predominance in labour-intensive sectors is another manifestation of this phenomenon.

Access. While the Nepalese poor, irrespective of gender, were still in the clutches of the village money lenders, more women than men lacked skills in dealing with credit institutions, faced bureaucratic difficulties in filling out forms, lacked connections with office personnel and lacked knowledge of the procedures for getting loans. Furthermore, land-ownership in Nepal is patrilineal by law thereby denying women access to land, which is a collateral for loans (ESCAP, 1981, p.67).

In Nepal, with the advent of the Green Revolution, women's role in farm management has become more significant (Pradhan, p.279). For non-labour farm management decisions, women make an overwhelming majority of the decisions concerning the Green Revolution technology inputs. For example, women make decisions concerning seed selection process (over 81 per cent of the decisions), use of improved seed (over 60 per cent of the decisions) and the amount and kind of fertilizer (nearly 40 per cent of the decisions by women as opposed to 32.5 per cent of the decisions by men). Men, on the other hand, make the majority of the decisions regarding labour allocation. This gender-based division of farm management responsibilities leaves in the hands of males an exploitative power of allocation of household labour. For example, Nepalese males systematically allocate the task of applying chemical fertilizers to themselves, relegating to women the unpleasant work of preparing and applying organic manure (Ahmed, 1987).

Lending to women should be given priority as evidence from Bangladesh reveals that 80 per cent of women's loans are utilized for processing and manufacturing and livestock and fisheries (Table 7). By contrast, men channel the bulk (61 per cent) of their loans into market-ing and trade. Clearly, the male borrowers increase traders' margins without helping the producer, and contribute to inflation (as their borrowing for service sector activities is not accompanied by an increase in the volume of production).

Social organization of production. From these discussions, it is evident that improved technologies, because of their sheer scale, would require reorganization of production from individual entrepreneurship to collective investment and operation. This has been successfully accom-plished in Bangladesh. Four women's groups (membership ranging from 30 to 40) have invested in rice mills during 1982–3 based on Grameen Bank loans (Abdullah 1984, p.216). In 1984 alone, 70 groups of land-less women secured Grameen Bank loans to operate rice hullers collec-tively. It is also remarkable in 1984 that 18 women's groups took loans for oil mills (Grameen Bank 1985, p.32). In addition, in 1984 landless women in Bangladesh took loans, through group formation, for High

Table 7: Disbursement of Grameen Bank loans to the landless population by gender and activity: Bangladesh, 1976 to 31 December 1984 (percentage of total)[a]

Gender	Landless males		Landless females	
Number and amount	No. of loans (total: 137,476)	Amount of loan (total: takas 280,544,825)	No. of loans (total: 137,242)	Amount of loan (total: takas 218,734,175)
Activity				
Processing & manufacturing	16	14	36	35
Agriculture & forestry	03	2	1	01
Livestock & fisheries	15	16	38	44
Services, trading, peddling & shopkeeping	50	61	14	16
Collective enterprises	16	7	11	04
Total (%)	100	100	100	100

[a] Source: Grameen Bank Annual Report, 1985, p.22

Yielding Varieties of rice cultivation (208 groups), fish farming (83 groups), livestock (88 groups) and poultry (20 groups).

In Pakistan, the Women's Milk Collection Association of Shah Jewna could improve their bargaining power through the formation of groups. Similarly, the informal work organizational forms in rice transplanting in India, which developed spontaneously, should be utilized for the establishment of formal grass roots organizations.

These scattered isolated experiences from South Asia confirm that women are more effectively mobilized for joint economic ventures, particularly those involving improved technologies, when they belong to similar class (landless households) or occupational (agricultural labourers, milk producers, weavers, etc.) backgrounds. On the one hand, the focus on shared class identities ideally encourages self reliance and motivates members to exert collective pressure on the wealthier members of the community for a larger share of material and social resources. On the other hand, this reveals that women from similar occupations can be more easily organized into co-operative work groups (e.g. for milk production in Pakistan) that transcend traditional socio-economic and political cleavages than it is for men.

A strategy for technology delivery

An ILO/Government of Norway project surveyed the range of technologies available for rural women in selected countries of Africa, and identified their preferences and priorities (ILO/Norway, 1984). On this basis, the ILO collaborated with the Ghana National Council for Women and Development (NCWD) to introduce improved technologies to 14 women's co-operative groups in six out of the country's ten regions in five processing activities (palm oil, soap, cassava, coconut oil and fish). These women's groups formed during 1977–84 ranged in membership from 12 to 43 women, each of whom was a shareholder (Ahmed, 1986).

This spontaneous adoption was due to the perceived advantages of the new technologies. For instance, the quantity of fish smoked by the improved Kagan oven was four-and-a-half times that of the traditional cylindrical oven. Moreover, loss due to the breakage of fish during the reshuffling of trays on the Kagan oven is insignificant compared with the traditional one. Similarly, the improved soap processing technology was readily adopted by the women's groups because (a) the volume of soap produced was higher (500 bars per day as compared with 100–150 bars by traditional methods); (b) it saves fuel, and hence production cost; and (c) it is safer, as there is no foaming-over during boiling and discharge into the moulding boxes.

Introduction of the new technologies has generated new or additional sources of income for 252 women in fish smoking, 75 women in palm oil production, 60 women in *gari* processing, 63 women in soap making and 30 women in coconut-oil production. These technologies have also reduced the arduousness (e.g., the pounding of palm fruits) of work of a total 440 women. The social organization of production based on women's co-operatives has been effective in the financial viability of the enterprises, reflected by their willingness to purchase shares from the co-operatives.

The sizes of the women's groups were geared to the scale of the improved technologies; there were, for example, smaller groups for fish smoking and segments of the labour processes in cassava, compared to larger groups for soap and palm oil. A sample survey of the women's groups shows that (a) composition of the groups is egalitarian in terms of ethnic origin, education, marital status, income and age, (b) at the individual level, drudgery is reduced and the time released is used for relaxation, child-care and higher participation in communal activities (church groups and literary classes), and (c) at the household level women contribute more to household expenditure.

The women take pride in both the income generated in the community (even for the men through backward production linkages) and the labour contributed to the processing unit. More importantly, one observes the emergence and strengthening of participatory democracy that is enshrined in the weekly meetings of the women's groups, at which every member has an equal right to speak her mind. This is a considerable advance on the traditional methods of village decision-making in which women did not feature very prominently.

The project also revealed that women could very easily operate powered machinery, the diesel engine in palm oil processing for example, and had shown greater concern for safety and health considerations, as they had children around.

Representatives of women's groups were trained at the Technology Consultancy Centre in Kumasi (the source of the improved technology) at the special training centre for soap-processing. These women in turn trained other members of their respective groups. The project helped establish and strengthen collaborative linkages among R and D institutions, manufacturers, extension services, financial institutions and women's groups (end-users of technology).

The lessons learned regarding the organization and strengthening of women's groups, and the insights obtained into their capacity to manage, operate and control improved technology are significant, and could be multiplied in other projects and countries. The following points are relevant in this process: (a) a project of this type should take care to make contact with potential users well before the projected date for adoption of the technology. Investigation of the technical skills, and the organizational and capital position of the women should be completed before it is announced to the women's group; (b) preparatory work with participating groups should begin well in advance, and should represent a substantial proportion of the total training time. Basic group and skill formation can take place before new equipment is made available; (c) extensive consultation with the women's groups should precede both their agreement to participate and the project's agreement to assist them. By discussing their own priorities and needs with such groups, project staff ensure that the users actually want the specific equipment and that it comes high, preferably first, in the appropriate sequence of their needs; and (d) documenting the list of leaders, office-bearers and members of women's groups and their formal registration will help prevent outsiders from taking over late, when the prospective benefits of the new technology make control attractive.

Consumption-oriented technologies
The vast majority of the cookstoves used in the South Asian countryside are 'chulas'. The chulas range in sophistication from crude pits, hollows in the ground, to fired clay and metal designs. The poor usually have one rudimentary chula with very low efficiency, e.g. between three to ten per cent in India (Batliwala, 1983). Similarly, the wood collected by an African woman is burned on a traditional three-stone fire place which has an efficiency ranging from five to ten per cent (Ligunyu, 1986). Typically a poor woman in the Third World has little access to cooking fuel, spends the longest time obtaining it, puts it to use in stoves which

are fuel-inefficient and time-consuming, and also subject her to smoke-related infections of the eye and respiratory systems.

Several improved models of 'smokeless' chulas are available in different regions of South Asia. For example, in the Indian Punjab a prototype developed by an architect jointly with village women attained fuel savings of 50 per cent. The chula ('Nada') was cheap and could be built and adapted by local women. Another prototype ('Dholadhar') developed in Himachal Pradesh had similar properties. Similarly, R and D is in progress in south India (Batliwala, 1983). In Bangladesh, a smokeless prototype chula which reduces fuel needs by one half has been developed in the Institute of Fuel Research and Development of the Bangladesh Council for Scientific and Industrial Research, but little progress has been made in its commercialization and use.

Despite the significant advantages of such consumption-oriented technologies, they are less likely to be adopted because the household can continue to expropriate unpaid, readily available female labour, while these technologies would need cash investments. One solution could be the mass production of such smokeless chulas, so that the complete stoves, or at least those critical components which require rigid adherence to technical dimensions could be marketed at subsidized prices. This would need to be simultaneously supported by collateral-free credit.

However, the problem of increasing the efficiencies of firewood chulas was not a non-trivial one, and demanded the insights of a combination of engineering, heat transfer and furnace design (Reddy and Reddy, 1983). For successful dissemination it may be necessary to mass produce such models and sell them at subsidized prices to the resource-poor households.

The smokeless chula is an innovation from several standpoints. It (a) cuts the fuel consumption by one half, reducing fuel-collection burden; (b) drastically reduces smoke-related diseases of the eye and respiratory systems; and (c) reduces time both for fuel collection and, through higher efficiency, lowers the time spent in the kitchen for cooking.

An improved wood-burning stove that uses only two pieces of fire-wood is not readily accepted in Kenya as the smoke from the traditional stove acted as an insect repellant and a reinforcement for strengthening the roofs (Ligunuya, 1986).

Energy technologies
One of the oldest alternatives to both traditional and commercial working fuels is biogas. It would be an ideal fuel for women: fast, efficient and clean cooking fuel, causing no health hazard. The energy yield from biogas is much greater than from using dung directly, as is very common in South Asia; the energy efficiency of cow dung cakes is about 11 per

70

cent compared to 60 per cent for biogas (Tucker 1983).[7] The Government of India is promoting its use: 75,000 units were installed in 1983, and another 75,000 were proposed that year (Batliwala 1983). Cost has been a major constraint (Rs.9,000 for a plant) and its adoption has been confined to rich households. The biogas plant prototype developed by the Fuel Research Institute is available in Bangladesh but this, like the Indian biogas technology, needs to be technically perfected and cost reductions achieved.

In Nepal, apart from considerations of liberating the women from excessive calorie expenditure, firewood shortage has directly contributed to the entire family's under-nutrition. A shortage of firewood has forced people to shift from two cooked meals a day, to one. (Arnold 1978, p.13).

In Nepal two different locally produced biogas technologies are available.[8] The drum-designed technology of three different scales (200 cubic feet to 500 cubic feet) is the most expensive (Table 8). The drumless or dome-designed biogas technology (particularly those smaller in scale) is more affordable. Dissemination rate for the 350 cubic feet capacity dome has been the highest because it has the lowest installation cost, lower operating costs (smaller amounts of dung) and the outputs are enough for the family needs (Khoju, 1984, p.20).

Table 8: Installation costs of biogas plants in Nepal: by level of technology and capacity[a]

Technology	Scale (cubic feet)	Costs (in Nepalese Rupees)
Drum	200	19,031
	350	29,031
	500	37,515
Dome	350	10,246
	530	14,990
	700	22,100

[a] Source: Khoju, 1984, p.50

To promote the use of biogas, the Agricultural Development Bank of Nepal extends loans for installation of plants. It financed 99 per cent of the 942 plants installed by 1982–3. The growth in annual installations has been steady. For instance, in 1982–3, 325 gas plants were installed as compared to 126 in 1978–9.

Apart from visual inspection, the manufacturer does not need to follow other quality control measures. However, the digester pit and gas

71

storage tank are provided guarantees for seven years, while the pipe, lamp, etc. are for one year only. Little effort is being made (a) to lower cost of installation; (b) to alternate feeds to the plant; (c) to improve the performance of accessories; (d) to improve gas formation in winter; and (e) to improve slurry use in crop cultivation. In Pakistan, a family of four to five members could save nearly Rs.2,000 annually by using a biogas plant of three cubic metres as against the conventional kerosene cookstove (ATDO, undated).

South-south co-operation
Apart from the North supporting the countries of the South in technology programmes, there is tremendous potential from mutually beneficial technical co-operation among developing countries (TCDC) themselves. Since there is a lack of an institutional framework for such co-operation, the North could play an important role in initiating and promoting such collaboration. For instance, a survey of the TCDC donor capacity of seven African countries revealed a very high potential for regional co-operation in respect of farm equipment innovations (ILO/FAO, 1985). In fact, the lack of such co-operation has led to a duplication of R and D efforts, the absence of regional trade, the emergence of excess capacity in farm equipment manufacturing in some of the countries, and higher costs for items imported from outside the region.

Here are some of the national initiatives (both technological and institutional in nature) which could make each of the following countries a net TCDC-donor in the field of mechanical innovations in agriculture (ILO/FAO, 1985):

Botswana

o Integration of the externally-funded Arable Land Development Programme into the organizational structure of the Department of Agricultural Field Services of the Ministry of Agriculture, supported by the country's own resources.
o Integrated Pilot Farming Project which provided extension support to farmers and assisted in the testing of R and D results in farmers' fields, similarly integrated into the organizational structure of DAFS.
o Evaluation of Farming Systems and Agriculture Implements Project, which originated as an externally funded project is also being integrated into the Ministry's Department of Research as new Farm Machinery Development Unit through an evolutionary process.
o Successfully tested and widely disseminated prototypes of equipment innovations like single-row standard planter, plough-mounted planter, planter fertilizer and cultivators.
o Rural Industries Innovation Centre, which also began as an

72

externally financed project now integrated with the Ministry of Industries as the nation's industrial training and extension centre.

Tanzania

o Successful industrial extension approaches to different categories and scales of manufacturing viz. (a) National Development Corporation assisting the large scale sector; (b) Metals Engineering Industries Development Association assisting the metal working industries (e.g. Cotex Metals, Vitanda Mfg. and Simon Mfg.); (c) Small Industries Development Organization assisting the village blacksmiths and the small-scale sector (e.g. Themi Farm Implements Co. and Industrial Estates, Mbeya.)
o Farm equipment prototype like the higher multi-purpose wooden beam tool frame which reduces costs to farmers and reduces the need for imported metal in its fabrication.
o Animal-drawn implement prototypes like inter-row cultivator, spike-tooth wooden-frame harrow, Mali planter, Kifarm two-furrow ox-drawn plough, two-furrow plough with seed attachment developed and tested in the Centre for Agricultural Mechanization and Rural Technology, Arusha (CAMERTEC).
o Hand-operated equipment prototypes like CAMERTEC hand planter.

Zambia

o Manufacturing capacity in factory-scale and village blacksmith levels for hand tools.
o Innovative industrial extension approach (FAO village workshop project) focusing on craftsmen for hand tools, hand weeders, wheel barrows, push carts.
o Village Industries Services geared to industrial extension support to small producers in rural areas.
o Prototype University of Zambia rotary injection planter.

Ethiopia

o The R and D model provided by the Agricultural Implements Research and Improvement Centre, capable of replication.
o The practical linkages between institutional and technological innovations in terms of scale. For instance (a) the Peasant Associations rely on hand tools and animal-drawn equipment; (b) the Producers Co-operatives because of collectivization (pooling) of land offer scope for intermediate-scale powered technologies; and (c) the large-scale sector linked to the use of large-scale capital-intensive technologies (80–90 h.p) and combines.

73

o The model of industrial extension and support to small-scale industries by the Handicrafts and Small-Scale Industries Agency and the role of Rural Skill Centres equipped with rudimentary equipment and facilities for the production of simple items and repair and maintenance.

o The unused scope for effective utilization of private dealers and service co-operatives for the distribution and marketing of agricultural tools and equipment.

o The Arrsi Rural Development Unit which originated as an externally funded project is now replicated through the institutionalization of this experiment in eight administrative zones; this approach integrates R and D, extension and training, manufacturing and financing of selected farm implements.

o A concrete practical illustration of the feasibility of involving the farmers in the modification of prototypes to more closely correspond to their needs, serves as a model for the region.

Kenya

o A successful initiative of R and D followed by rigorous extension and training at the farmer training centres bringing the farmers into technical and organizational readiness for receiving equipment innovations.

o Illustrations of sustained R and D, farmer training and promotion of local manufacture in a systematic fashion and phased sequence.

o Factory-scale manufacturing capacity in hand tools and ploughs.

o Promotion of small-scale industries through infrastructure support such as the Kenya Industrial Estates.

o Prototypes of multi-purpose ox-plough permitting use of a variety of attachments ranging from plough, weeder, harrows, ridger, potato lifter and ground-nut lifter.

o Prototype rotary punch planter pushed by one operator with versatility to cover a diverse range of soil conditions, making it amenable for transfer to Network countries.

o Prototype hand-pushed wheel hoe for weeding maize and other crops.

o Lessons learned in bottle-necks of inter-Ministerial co-ordination (e.g. commercial manufacture farm equipment innovations delayed by bureaucratic rigidities of Central Tendering Board).

Sudan

o Gigantic strides made in the large-scale rain-fed and mechanized farming sectors and the corresponding problems of repair, maintenance and replacement of obsolete machinery.

74

o The virtual neglect of the dominant traditional agricultural sub-sector which has given rise to a technological dualism and impoverishment of the subsistence farm families and emergence of regional disparities.

o Research and development efforts on animal-drawn implements in the Nuba mountains and Sag-el-Naam areas.

o The participation of financial institutions (Agricultural Bank of Sudan) in the direct import and marketing of agricultural machinery and the associated problems of competition of parastatals with the private importers and distributors.

From this review, certain strategies for development co-operation in technology stand out. Contrary to the popular perception in many Third World countries that increased efficiency is definitely associated with higher capital intensity (Singer, 1979), ILO work has established that intermediate technologies available in agriculture, forestry and women's processing activities in rural areas can be labour-using. In addition to generating productive employment, these intermediate technologies offer in varying degrees the advantages of improved working conditions. Typically, the application of these intermediate technologies leads to increased productivity when compared with traditional techniques, but decreased labour displacement compared with the more capital-intensive ones.

The modest ILO operational programme reveals that technologies selectively picked from this fairly rich stock of intermediate alternatives can be disseminated directly to the target groups by working through their participatory organizations at the grass roots level. This approach of direct delivery of technology at the grass roots level has a learning effect on the national developmental institutions who act as counterpart bodies to such externally managed but jointly executed pilot projects. This mechanism of channelling improved technologies directly to target groups could ensure that a larger proportion of benefits reaches these groups as against the traditional 'trickle down' approach.

Due account has to be taken of the sex-sequential nature of the labour process of production linkages in selected industries. The strengthening of such backward and forward linkages could significantly contribute to mass employment and income for women, eventually contributing to poverty alleviation in rural areas.

Priority should be given on a collateral-free basis to women borrowers who have productively utilized the credit (with high repayment rates), particularly to groups which make collective investments in rice mills, vegetable oil mills, fish smoking, cassava processing, etc., both in Asia and Africa. While this will ease constraints of vital working- and fixed-capital requirements, the provision of risk capital is critical if women's

75

livelihood is to be preserved. The few scattered and isolated illustrations of women's groups improving both their domestic (control over income) and external (protecting and increasing earning opportunities) bargaining power, need support. Every opportunity should be siezed to build formal organizational structures for women based on the informal and spontaneous social organization of production, as in Bangladesh and Ghana.

Consumption-oriented technologies deserve high priority not only to liberate women from the high human-energy intensive nature of domestic work, but also to assist households on the brink of starvation for want of cooking fuel, as in Nepal. Here too, energy technologies like biogas could play as critical a role as inexpensive fuel-efficient smokeless stoves (reducing women's risks from respiratory and eye diseases).

Finally, collective self-reliance in technology among Third World countries can be achieved through South-South co-operation. The concrete possibility of TCDC presented for a sub-region from Africa deserves external support from the North, simply because of the lack of institutional framework to translate this potential into a viable reality.

Institutional aspects of Appropriate Technology

MARILYN CARR
Policy Planning Unit, ITDG

THE PROCESS of technology development and diffusion is highly complex, and one of the major factors influencing its success or failure is the quality of the institution or institutions involved in implementing or promoting it. Given their crucial role, it is surprising that so little attention is given to appraising the strengths and weaknesses of the various types of institution and that so little is known about the nature of the institutional framework most likely to promote the sustained development and diffusion of AT in particular circumstances.

Institutional issues need to be considered at two levels: that of project implementation including experimental, pilot, demonstration and dissemination phases; and that of autonomous development and diffusion outside the project environment.

Project implementation
At the level of project implementation, two major questions arise:

o What types of organizations (and individuals) can help in implementing Appropriate Technology programmes, and what are the strengths and weaknesses of each?

o What institutional arrangements can be made to combine the strengths of some or all of these groups in the service of AT development and diffusion?

Simply put: who is best at doing what, and how can they all be brought together?

Stages in the development and diffusion of AT
To answer these questions it is useful to examine the normal phases through which an Appropriate Technology project passes. Figure 1 suggests there are six major phases in a project's life, each of which demands a different mix of skills, expertise and inputs.

Identification of needs, markets and resources. This first phase in an AT project is the most crucial of all since if it is not done properly or if it is neglected altogether (as often happens in technology projects) any effort and resources devoted to later stages can be totally wasted. All too often a technology is designed in a vacuum without due

77

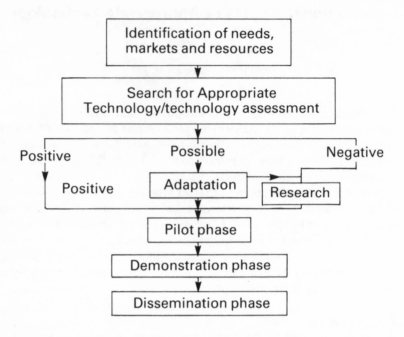

Figure 1. Stages in the process of development and diffusion of AT

consideration being given to whether anyone needs or wants it or can afford to buy or use it.

It is important, therefore, to start with the perceived needs and wants of intended beneficiaries, to differentiate clearly between needs and wants, and to verify whether wants can be backed up by purchasing power. This latter point is particularly important when dealing with groups such as rural women who normally have very limited access to cash income or credit.

The careful exploration of circumstances at the start of a project will help to guard against incidents of trying to introduce 'improved' technologies which do not meet a priority need, do not conform with socio-cultural patterns, or do not improve at all on the traditional method of doing things. It will also help to define where constraints in the traditional technology or technique arise and to get some economic parameters on the required technology. In cases where the aim is to increase the productivity of existing enterprises or to establish new ones, it will indicate whether raw material, skill and energy requirements will be available, and whether markets are likely to exist for the output and at what price.

78

The potential beneficiaries need to be fully involved in the process of defining their own needs and wants. Only in this way will the staff of external assistance agencies be able to identify or develop a technology which will be acceptable and of use to intended users.

Technology search and appraisal. Having identified a need for an improved technology and having set some basic parameters on the nature of the technology required, the second phase involves searching for a solution.

There are many sources of information now available on the range of technologies in existence. In some countries, there may be a catalogue of technologies available locally, or an institution which can provide information on what is available within the country. If a search of locally available technologies proves unsuccessful, then the search needs to be extended further afield — first to other countries in the region and then to other parts of the world. Again, catalogues are available to assist in this process and there are several regional and international institutions which can be consulted for information and advice.

Rarely do technologies need to be developed from scratch, as it is usually possible to identify an existing technology which more or less approximates to the one required.

Technology adaptation. Although it will usually be possible to find a technology which is more or less what is being asked for, it will nearly always be necessary to adapt this to some extent to take account of differing circumstances. For instance, a fish-smoking oven from West Africa may have to be adapted before use in Kenya to allow for differences in required taste and quality of the final product. The information upon which to base decisions regarding adaptation should have been collected during the first phase of the project. Further consultations with potential users may be necessary, however, to decide the extent of technical work required to arrive at an appropriate solution. This may vary from minor technical adjustments to more major research tasks.

Pilot phase. Following adaptation, the new technology can be tested technically in the laboratory or workshop in which adaptation has taken place. This will reveal whether the device or process can stand up to typical situations such as damage by, for example, animals, children or the weather, as through inexperienced operators or overuse. It will also help to establish whether the required levels and quality of raw materials are available, and whether the product can be produced at any acceptable price and quality.

During this phase, the involvement of the intended beneficiaries is crucial since they can apply their knowledge to that of the technologists to assist in the process of further refining the technology to match local circumstances.

79

Demonstration phase. Having ascertained that the technology actually works in one village and is of use to and accepted by a small number of intended beneficiaries, there is then a need to demonstrate the viability of the technology in a wider range of circumstances.

The demonstration phase of a project basically serves three major functions:

o it shows that a particular technology can be applied over a wide area;

o it proves to consumers/users that they will benefit from the technology, thus persuading them to invest in it; and

o it shows potential suppliers of the technology that a market exists and that it is worthwhile investing in production.

Experience in introducing appropriate technologies such as ceramic stoves in several countries has shown that many thousands of such goods may need to be distributed free to households before users and producers become convinced of their worth or viability. Engaging in an exercise such as this obviously requires considerable funds from support agencies.

Dissemination phase. Project implementation cannot normally end with demonstrating the viability of an improved technology: intervention will often still be necessary to test full-scale production technology, and to organize an effective delivery system for inputs and outputs. There are basically two major approaches to diffusion — the extension approach, and the commercial approach, both of which will need testing out before further project involvement can be deemed to be unnecessary.

For example, if the extension approach is thought appropriate, there will be a need to see if government extension services will be able to cope with new demands placed on them beyond a confined demonstration phase, or whether further intervention is required in the form of training, or vehicles, for example. Similarly, if the commercial approach is thought to be appropriate, there will be a need to see if commercial financing systems are willing and able to provide the producer and consumer credit required on the necessary scale, and to identify if there are any policy constraints on the diffusion of the technology.

Institutional strengths and weaknesses
To return then to our original question as to who is best at doing what, it should be clear from this argument that different types of institution will be more or less useful in different combinations during different phases of a project's life.

Local farmers, entrepreneurs and artisans. For the most part, these people are the social carriers, and the intended beneficiaries, of

Appropriate Technology and they have much knowledge and skill to contribute to the development and diffusion of Appropriate Technology. As was seen in the previous section, effective diffusion requires their active involvement and participation in most phases of an Appropriate Technology project. All too often, however, they are not consulted or enabled to participate in their own development because of the 'top-down' methods of many implementing agencies and because of factors (such as lack of transport facilities or inability of male extension workers to reach rural women) which inhibit effective communication. Methods need to be found to draw on this otherwise wasted resource.[1]

One way in which this can be done is through assisting farmers or artisans to form their own organizations which can then take their rightful place in the development process. One such organization is the South India Federation of Fishermen's Societies, in Trivandrum, which seeks to give technical and marketing advice and assistance to the 2,000 artisanal fishermen who comprise its membership. Another is the Self Employed Women's Association in Ahmedabad which has a membership of thousands of rural and urban poor women who rely on the Association for a range of technical and financial services aimed at increasing the productivity of their work. Organizations such as this have proved a useful channel between the poor, the technology, and the development assistance agencies which seek to assist them, and they provide a means by which the ideas and opinions of the poor can be properly incorporated in the process of technology development and diffusion.

Local non-governmental organizations. Local NGOs also have a very important part to play in Appropriate Technology projects. Many are based in the rural and urban slum areas and most have dedicated staff who have lived and worked with the people they seek to assist for many years. As such, they are normally very sensitive to the needs of the rural and urban poor, and have a good understanding of the type of assistance measures which are most beneficial. Their heaviest involvement in technology projects is normally at the crucial first stage of needs identification, and they are usually fully involved also in the pilot phase, with decreasing influence thereafter.

There are of course many types of local NGO ranging from those which have no technological expertise of their own to those which incorporate technology units. Examples of the former include the Bangladesh Rural Advancement Committee, and the Sarvodaya Movement in Sri Lanka, both of which rely heavily on staff from other agencies to supply the technical inputs which are needed during project implementation. Examples of the latter include Dian Desa in Indonesia, and the Rural Industries Innovation Centre in Botswana, which can handle both technical and non-technical aspects of projects and have a correspondingly lesser need to buy in outside technical assistance.

The examples given are all well-funded agencies which are well connected with national and international sources of information and expertise. There are, of course, millions of very small local NGOs which are equally aware of the needs of the communities with which they work, but which have very limited access to sources of technological knowledge or expertise. This problem can be partially overcome by forming linkages between large and small groups — as is the case with Dian Desa and a multitude of smaller NGOs in Indonesia. It can also be partially overcome by the formation of an 'umbrella' technology centre which can seek out and respond to the needs of all types of development agencies.[1]

However, even the larger NGOs often lack sufficient technical/ commercial competence or financial resources of their own to sustain Appropriate Technology projects or to replicate their work beyond a small area. Thus, while they may be able to implement a project as far as the pilot phase, without undue reliance on other agencies, they must usually seek to collaborate with a variety of other institutions to get beyond this stage.

Research institutions and technology centres. There are a number of different types of research and development centres in Third World countries ranging from those in the formal sector, which have no interest in or capacity to do anything about the needs of the rural and urban poor, to those which have been established by government, universities or NGOs with the specific purpose of working on Appropriate Technology.[2]

While in the long term it would be valuable to have all institutions addressing themselves to the technologies needed by the poor, there is little involvement at the moment of formal research institutes in Appropriate Technology projects. This section concentrates, therefore, on centres which work mainly on the identification, adaptation and testing of ATs.

Government centres include the Appropriate Technology Development Organization in Pakistan. University-based centres include the Technology Consultancy Centre in Ghana, the Development Technology Centre in Indonesia, the Research Centre for Applied Science and Technology in Nepal, and the Appropriate Technology Development Institute in Papua New Guinea. In addition to the several NGOs which have established technology units in support of their work with communities, a few have established a focus primarily on technology research and development. One such example is the Appropriate Technology Development Association in India.[3]

A problem for many of these centres is that they tend to be distanced from the rural and urban poor who they are supposed to be assisting, with the result that the all-important involvement of potential beneficiaries in the development process does not occur. Technologists have found to their cost that technologies designed in a vacuum rarely prove useful to or get adopted by intended beneficiaries. Some have gone on to find ways of overcoming this problem by establishing off-shoot technology development units in the midst of the communities they wish to assist. One very successful example of this is the TCC in Ghana which, having found difficulty in commercializing its technologies while located on the campus of the University of Science and Technology in Kumasi has proceeded to establish Intermediate Technology Transfer Units in the heart of the informal sector, in Kumasi and elsewhere.[4]

NGO technology centres normally start with closer links to intended beneficiaries (although this is not always the case). However, they are less likely than government or university-based centres to have a comprehensive range of in-house technical skills. They are also less likely to have access to expensive laboratory equipment. Their strength, therefore, lies in minor technical adaptation and field testing rather than in more major technology development work.

Commercial companies both in developed and developing countries can play a part in the development and dissemination of Appropriate Technology in the Third World if it is in their financial interests to do so. Sometimes, a commercial company is commissioned by a development agency to design a new device or process. For example, ITDG has commissioned small companies in the UK to work on electronic load controllers for use in micro hydro projects in Nepal, and on improved boat-building materials and designs for use in fishery projects in south India. Commercial companies may invest their own resources in R and D if the market potential seems great enough: a number of small private companies in Nepal have been involved in developing various types of water-powered devices to meet varying needs of rural communities for shaft power. Normally, however, it is left to development assistance agencies to initiate and implement the projects which establish that a market exists in the first place.

The main involvement of commercial companies in Appropriate Technology projects comes at the pilot, demonstration and dissemination phase. Here they are useful to test out and demonstrate prototype processes designed by Technology Centres (something they are willing to do if the new process promises to lead to increased profits). They are also often vital during the demonstration and dissemination phases for the production of an adequate supply of the appropriate technology being promoted. It is surprising how many Appropriate Technology projects are started without any thought being given to how the producer or consumer goods involved will be produced and distributed in the event that demand for them is stimulated.

Commercial banks and other financing institutions. These are important during the dissemination (and sometimes even the demonstration) phase of a project to provide the fixed and working capital needed for the promotion of Appropriate Technology activities. Often, their standard financing methods and appraisal techniques cannot accommodate the specific needs and conditions of small, decentralized rural enterprises, village artisans or women's groups, and the involvement of a development agency will usually be necessary before loans are forthcoming from normal commercial sources.

The extent to which a development agency will need to involve itself in gearing up sources of credit will depend partly on the commitment of commercial banks to rural and informal sector development, and the availability of dispersed banking facilities. It will also depend partly on the nature of the technology being diffused and the size and location of the production units needing loans. In the case of technologies such as small rural mills or soap manufacturing plants, the development agency may need to support the first few installations, so that data on financial viability can be secured to help with getting commercial credit for future installations. The development agency may also be called on by the bank to act as guarantor for loans to small enterprises investing in new processes.

Generally, the more remote and smaller the enterprise and the poorer the prospective borrower, the greater the need will be for development agency involvement. In some cases, this may extend to the development agency having to set up its own 'bank' as a project in its own right. One example of this is the famous Grameen Bank project in Bangladesh which lends to the landless and assetless members of society (many of them women) to enable them to participate in productive activity. By proving that it is both possible and profitable to lend money to the poor, it is hoped eventually to make all banking facilities in the country more responsive to their needs.

Government departments and agencies. Central and regional governments can play a role in Appropriate Technology projects at several levels. First, they have vast resources of buildings, transport, equipment and extension personnel that can be used in needs identification as well as pilot, demonstration and dissemination phases of a project. Their effectiveness obviously varies from place to place, but generally problems are experienced in covering remote communities, and government personnel are usually not so likely to develop long-term working relationships with the rural and urban poor as are staff of NGOs. In some countries, however, there are very few NGOs in existence,

84

and government workers may be the only source of information on community needs and the only method of transferring a new technology or technique to more than one or two communities.

Second, governments may establish Appropriate Technology committees or co-ordinating centres which can act as a focus for Appropriate Technology promotion within the country. These differ from the Government Technology Centres mentioned earlier in that they are involved mainly in information gathering, and dissemination and linking diverse agencies within the country which have an interest and involvement in implementing Appropriate Technology projects. There are now Appropriate Technology committees in countries such as Malawi, Zambia, Sierra Leone and Tanzania, while the Bostwana government has a Technology Centre which acts as the main focus for Appropriate Technology in the country. Such committees and co-ordinating centres play an important role in liaising with international Appropriate Technology centres and in identifying and assessing technology options.

Third, governments may be useful in removing constraints experienced during the dissemination phase of a project. For example, the Kenyan government has been able to assist a local NGO (KENGO) with the dissemination phase of an improved stoves project by legalizing the position of the artisans producing the stoves, thus allowing them to work more productively and without harrassment on city council land.[5] Similarly, the Nepal government has helped during the dissemination phase of a micro hydro project by changing its policy to permit the private generation and sale of electricity up to a 100kw limit.[6]

International NGOs. There are many international NGOs which have an active interest and involvement in implementing Appropriate Technology projects. Most of these (for example Oxfam, Save the Children, IDRC, Bread for the World) have a general rural development, a small enterprise focus, while others (e.g. ITDG, Appropriate Technology International, GRET, COTA) have a specific focus on Appropriate Technology. Still others are volunteer organizations (Peace Corps, VSO, CUSO, Norwegian and Dutch volunteer organizations) which frequently supply technical volunteers to assist with the Appropriate Technology projects of field agencies.

Specialized Appropriate Technology institutions assist field agencies with the implementation of projects in a variety of ways. On request, they can normally assist with identification of appropriate technology solutions. Some can help with technology adaptation and provide techno-economic assistance during the pilot and demonstration phases of a project. Others can provide commercial advice or financial assistance to help overcome constraints during demonstration and dissemination. Still others provide more comprehensive services such as assistance to

85

project directors on designing and implementing all aspects of an Appropriate Technology project, or even helping to set up Appropriate Technology units within NGOs. For example, ITDG is assisting BRAC in Bangladesh to establish its own technology unit in support of its rural employment projects for the landless.

Bilateral and multilateral donor agencies. These can provide essential funds for Appropriate Technology projects, especially during the resource-intensive demonstration and dissemination phases. For example, World Bank and UN money has been useful in enabling national governments and local NGOs in various countries to demonstrate the viability of improved stoves by installing them free or at highly subsidized rates in thousands of households. Such agencies can also help enormously during the dissemination phase by earmarking loan funds specifically for the support of small rural enterprises, which are the social carriers of Appropriate Technology. For example, the Asian Development Bank has assisted local NGOs, private companies and the commercial bank in Nepal in this way through provision of a loan in support of the dissemination phase of a micro hydro project.

International agencies can also play an important role in developing local technical capabilities through support of local research institutes and the funding of vocational/technical training centres and programmes. Often, however, they promote technological dependency instead through tying aid to machinery and goods manufactured in First World countries.

Institutional framework

Successful implementation of an Appropriate Technology project involves bringing the strengths of all these various agencies together, helping to overcome their weaknesses, and establishing institutional relationships when necessary. Factors which need to be considered in this process include:

o criteria for choosing a focus agency which can co-ordinate all the various inputs and the methods by which this co-ordination can be achieved and maintained;
o method for implementing a truly collaborative approach to development, whereby knowledge travels up from the rural poor to the development agency, and the international agencies learn from and listen to local agencies, as well as the other way round.

These points are not unrelated since the choice of focus agency will, by and large, determine the extent to which a 'trickle-up' approach to project development and implementation is likely to occur.

For the main part, NGOs seem to make better focus agencies than research institutions/technology centres, government departments or commercial banks or companies — providing they have access to and can afford to buy in or can gear up any technical, financial or commercial components they lack themselves. Starting with their understanding of and commitment to poor communities, NGOs are much more likely to get projects off to a good start than most other institutions and they have more of an interest in seeing a project through to its desired end of widespread production and use of technologies by and for the poor.

Technology centres, being more remote from the poor, are prone to loose sight of the ultimate aim of an Appropriate Technology project and become engrossed by technical matters rather than seeking out needed socio-economic or commercial assistance. Commercial companies tend to have little interest in providing the demonstration and dissemination of technologies to other companies who will become competitors and reduce profits. There are, of course, exceptions to this, but NGOs do seem to have played the dominant role in most successful Appropriate Technology projects.

To demonstrate the importance of getting the institutional framework right, two examples of Appropriate Technology projects are given. In the first, the Small Turbine and Mill Projects in Nepal, an NGO (United Mission to Nepal) has acted as the focus agency. In the second, the Oil Press Project in Sierra Leone, the initial impetus came from a government department which proved to be a much weaker focus agency.

The Small Turbine and Mill Project (STMP), Nepal. [7]The United Mission to Nepal (UMN), a private voluntary organization composed of nearly 40 Protestant groups and church-related aid agencies, co-ordinates the STMP. The UMN has been active in both technical and non-technical aspects of micro hydro development. Its Social and Economic Planning Unit has carried out needs assessments and socio-economic analysis of areas where existing mechanical turbine mills could be upgraded to provide electricity for local villages and entrepreneurs. UMN's Butwal Technical Institute has produced turbines and provided engineering services for this upgrading (including civil, mechanical and electrical work), and has helped in training local people in micro hydro power plant design and construction.

But there has been far more to the STMP than just the dedicated work of the UMN. Important technical support has been provided from overseas groups in order to bring-state-of-the-art technology into the construction of simpler, more effective power systems. ITDG has provided electrical engineering innovations and assisted in the development of electronic load control systems, which simplify and reduce the costs of electricity generation. ITDG has been assisted in the latter area by a private British manufacturer, GP Electronics, which has designed the load controllers and licenced UMN to produce them. Another British company, Evans Engineering, has been working with ITDG on the design and production of multi-jet pelton wheels, and may licence and train UMN in their manufacture. These turbines would replace the present cross flow turbines in larger micro hydro installations, when UMN expands its programme to electrify larger villages and towns.

The Government of Nepal's policy support has been essential to the success of the STMP. It has decreed that no licence is required to generate and sell electricity below 100kw, which has permitted local mill owners to join the UMN electrification programme. The Agricultural Development Bank (with assistance from the Asian Development Bank) has provided low-interest loans for individuals and co-operatives for the installation of micro hydro equipment. Recently, the Government has made a subsidy of up to Rs100,000 for the purchase of electrification equipment. Basically, the Government of Nepal has decided to support the independent, private sector approach to rural electrification as the most viable option for small, remote village applications, and has used legal and other policy measures to provide incentives for increased activity by UMN and its collaborators in this area.

The development of micro hydro power in Nepal through STMP thus contains the productive combination of the resources of government and commercial banking facilities, local and international NGOs, local and overseas private enterprise and multilateral donor assistance in the design and implementation of rural electrification schemes. Technical, economic, social and policy measures all have contributed to the success of the project — and their implementation is due to the development of multi-institutional co-operation and collaboration in pursuit of the dissemination of this appropriate technology.

As a result of the UMN initiative, there are now at least seven local turbine manufacturers in Nepal. Thus, the nation has acquired not only the availability of an important technology, but also the capacity to produce and sustain that technology and its benefits.

The Oil Press Project, Sierra Leone.[8] A UN consultant visited Sierra Leone at the request of the Ministry of Social Welfare to investigate possibilities of improving traditional palm oil processing. The Ministry arranged visits to various parts of the country to talk to women involved in the industry and to see the process at first hand.

The traditional process appeared to be arduous, time-consuming and inefficient, and it seemed probable that improvements could be introduced which would increase the income earned by village women.

The Ministry of Social Welfare had no internal technical capacity and was uncertain as to which other agencies could provide the necessary assistance. One staff member thought that the university had some interest in Appropriate Technology and set up a meeting with the head of the Department of Mechanical Engineering. This proved to be a useful meeting since it was found that there was a small group of engineers at the university who belonged to an informal Appropriate Technology society. Among other things, they supervised and worked with students on designing technologies appropriate to the needs of the country. They were delighted to meet with the Ministry staff members who could tell them what needs existed as they had no resources to travel out of the capital city to see for themselves.

The UN consultant agreed to recommend for funding a project which involved:

- o a baseline survey by the Ministry in selected villages to determine the characteristics of an improved oil press;
- o the design of an oil press by the university in accordance with these specifications;
- o the production of a prototype by the university for testing in a village;
- o the production by the university of 32 oil presses for testing and demonstration in different locations;
- o the training of selected villagers in the use of the oil press;
- o monitoring of the progress of the project by the Ministry.

A number of problems arose during the course of the project. First, because the proposal did not specify that the university should participate in the baseline survey, this crucial step was left to the Ministry staff who were not trained in collecting the type of data relevant to technology design. As a result a prototype machine was designed which was too small, saved no time and was less profitable than the traditional method. As a result of the women's reaction to this prototype, some adjustments were made to try to improve the technology, and work was started on producing more presses for demonstration purposes.

At this stage, a second problem arose. The university staff were anxious to move on to new design projects for/or with their students, and found it difficult to tie up time and laboratory facilities in the production of oil presses. Schedules fell further and further behind and by the time the first six presses were ready, the peak time for oil processing had passed, making it difficult for Ministry workers to introduce them successfully to villages. In addition, the pressure of time made it difficult for university staff to fulfil their commitment to travel to the villages to help install the presses and to train women to use them. A compromise was reached which involved running a training course for Ministry workers and villagers at the university, but this was not very effective and, in any case, men came to the university rather than women.

The result was that all but one of the six presses were rejected by villagers, and severe problems were encountered with the sixth. Pressure from the UN donor agency helped in persuading the university to do some serious work on re-designing the press to overcome these problems, and eventually a satisfactory prototype was produced.

A final problem now arose. The university refused to become involved in the production of oil presses since it needed its facilities for design rather than production purposes. The Ministry was therefore forced to investigate the possibilities of getting the presses manufactured by commercial firms. They had little success in this venture because they had no experience in transferring the design from the university to the companies they contacted and no way of assessing what skills, equipment and labour would be required. In any case, the companies were not really interested because a market had not been established. In addition, while the university had been able to import small quantities of steel to make prototypes, the private sector was unable to acquire any steel at all because of a government ban on imports.

Beyond the project: the policy framework
While successful development projects can help hundreds and even thousands of poor people to acquire better standards of living, they are, at the end of the day, only projects. The masses of poor people in the Third World will never be able to benefit from project activities, and some other way must be found of enabling them to participate in and benefit from economic and social development.

The solution to this problem lies at the macro-level, with economic policies which affect the distribution of resources between sectors, and between the rich and the poor, as well as affecting decisions of technology choice in the private sector. For example, fiscal policies can be used to stimulate demand for those products which are normally produced by small-scale rather than large-scale industry, thus providing increased markets and incomes for the thousands of poor people who depend on small-scale industry for their livelihoods. Taxation or import policies can be used to reduce demand for mechanized farming equipment and to stimulate demand for the products of rural workshops instead. And, through credit distribution, investment can be directed towards the small-scale sector and away from the large-scale sector.

In addition, governments may direct publicly owned firms to take particular decisions or lay down the criteria public firms should adopt so that they favour appropriate technology choice. And, when processing development projects, governments need to give thought to the likely impact of the level of technology on output, employment and foreign exchange.

Subsidized capital and foreign exchange, as well as cheap energy and other infrastructural goods have led to the growth of the large-scale agricultural and industrial sectors in most countries at the expense of the small scale. Automated rice mills, tractors and capital-intensive food processing plants, and capital goods industries, have destroyed the livelihoods of millions of small producers and farm labourers. Only a firm commitment on the part of government to introduce and implement policy measures which reverse this trend will lead to a more sustainable pattern of development which benefits the poorer sectors of society as well as the better off.

But in many countries, there is no clear mechanism of assessing the impact of various policy measures on technology choice, or the implications of choosing a particular technology option for the economy as a whole. There are various institutional options for providing more effective choice: assessment units within planning ministries; assessment units within operational ministries; advisory committees; technology councils; and so on. But, while there is now sufficient experience of implementing appropriate technology projects to set out guidelines for establishing an appropriate institutional framework at the micro-level, no such guidelines exist at the macro-level.

Given the importance of 'getting beyond the project' there is an urgent need to undertake a much more thorough investigation of the ways in which technology choices are made in the public sector, as well as assessing the strengths and weaknesses of various institutional options for assessing the impact of economic policies on technology choice in the private sector.

Finally, note needs to be made of the effect which aid agencies have on the choice of technology in the projects that they finance.[9] Although there are examples of multilateral and bilateral support to major Appropriate Technology programmes (mainly rural roads, improved stoves, handpumps and water and sanitation), the policies of these donors have tended to favour the sort of capital-intensive, large-scale production systems which benefit an already well-off élite at the expense of the masses of the rural and urban poor. Any attempts on the part of Third World governments to improve the mechanisms for technology choice must be matched by a similar move on the part of donor agencies.

Summary

A major aim of the Appropriate Technology Movement is to enable the rural and urban poor to become (or stay) involved in the production and provision of those basic goods and services which are needed on a regular basis by most local communities.

To bring this about, action is required at two levels:

○ at the micro-level, methods need to be evolved by which various types of agencies are encouraged and enabled to collaborate with each other on the identification and implementation of effective AT projects which benefit the rural and urban poor on a sustained basis, and

○ at the macro-level, strategies need to be derived which encourage and enable Third World governments and multilateral and bilateral donors to adopt policies which encourage small-scale versus large-scale agriculture, labour-intensive versus capital-intensive infra-structural development, and the promotion of small-scale decent-ralized industrial activity in rural areas.

The two are not unrelated, since successful projects are useful in convincing policy makers that alternative development strategies might be worth adopting. Unless they do assist in bringing about necessary changes at the policy level, however, the impact of Appropriate Technology projects in themselves will remain limited.

Closing address

STEINAR SKJAEVELAND

Director-General, The Royal Norwegian Ministry of Development Co-operation

DURING THESE two days we have used many phrases for the 'technology' we are talking about — 'intermediate', 'appropriate', 'suitable', 'right technology at the right time' — the child has many names, and it is difficult to find a good definition covering what we mean at any given time. I prefer the notion of 'appropriate' technology depending on the problem you want to solve.

We discovered, however, that we could talk meaningfully about many types of technology, defining this concept broadly. To me, technology is basically a tool to help create development towards certain agreed overall goals. But the choice of technology is not neutral. The choice of technology is important in deciding what type of development, and for whom. It is important to put people, human needs, in the centre. 'Design for need' is therefore a good slogan.

Technical solutions are one thing, technology is something much more. A technology contains, among others, social, economic and environmental aspects, and the cross-cultivation of sciences. It must work within all the limitations of a developing country, and must assist in fulfilling the overall aims of that society and the specific aims of a development project.

We seem to agree that often the best solution is to be found in local technology with, when necessary, something being added to this. Sometimes of course it is necessary to find a completely new technology. An example might be offshore oil drilling. The appropriate technology in such a situation is what is called 'high' technology. Still it is 'appropriate' to solve such a task. If new technology must be added, the question of the transfer of the technology arises, with new sets of challenges to the recipient as well as the donor. A NORAD research programme is already under way to shed light on the issues facing both parties to such transfers.

The importance of the right *attitudes* has been mentioned several times. Attitudes on both sides, because there might be limitations of culture, communication, knowledge on both sides. It was agreed that the solutions must be acceptable also in economic terms. Economics is the science of scarce resources, and resources are always scarce — now more than ever. The importance of good and cheap economic solutions will increase in the future.

More emphasis than ever is being put on the environment, because we want sustainable development. Easy solutions using natural resources uneconomically and destroying the future chance of survival is not

93

acceptable. The UN Commission on the Environment will, we hope, have an important contribution to make on this matter in the future.

Employment is an important aim in itself for both human and social reasons, and because we must utilize human resources to the maximum to create growth. Employment is also important because of income distribution effects, which again will have political impact.

Integration and *participation* are important aspects of Norwegian aid policy. This means that important target groups, such as the women, must be brought into the decision-making process when a choice of technology is made. This can be done more efficiently using intermediate technology, based on local knowledge.

As has been pointed out there now is more knowledge, experience — and good ideas — than ever. On the other hand the situation in many countries of the Third World is getting more desperate every day. But the total picture is not entirely gloomy: many countries have been able to start on the road to increased growth and enhanced social conditions. The situation is a great challenge to all of us. It is a time of opportunity because old solutions are being scrapped and demands for new ones are being made. Solutions with better effects on target groups, and which use resources more economically, are actively asked for. In Norwegian aid policy these are the untried elements of the sustainable development we have talked about. Sustainable development for poorer groups, for women, for the environment, for employment — this is our goal. There is also active work on certain concrete projects/sectors. We now must develop an overall strategy to deal with both political goals and concrete project objectives, a way of dealing with both development and development assistance.

The timing of this seminar is therefore most appropriate. The increased interest and enthusiasm which I feel is present must not be allowed to fade away. Perhaps our own society, too, will need some of the same solutions. What we need is long-term sustainable solutions adapted for people on their own levels of development. Planning and organizing such solutions based on Appropriate Technology and making them work is a great challenge. This is because such solutions are by no means simpler or less complex. They might be more complex to organize, for instance, for they often need new skills and different inputs.

We shall need ITDG's co-operation also in the future. Let us establish a network of contacts and let us work to exchange ideas and experience. Maybe we should establish a focal point that can spearhead this development. We have little capacity at present and our quality of assistance is not good enough.

On behalf of the Ministry I thank the Norwegian Society of Chartered Engineers and the Intermediate Technology Group for a very interesting and well organized seminar. Thank you very much.

Appendix 1   Issue papers

Group 1: Priorities for Appropriate Technology (AT) intervention through development assistance programmes

Technologies exist (or can be developed) which are appropriate to the needs and circumstances of all sections of society. With which people should AT programmes be concerned and what are the technologies which are appropriate to their needs?

Who should benefit?

Generally, AT interventions aim to help the poor. But who are the poor? Those people with the lowest cash income in a country are not always the most deprived or the most in need. And should one work first with the poorest of the poor, who have the least resources to contribute to AT development, or instead work with those with limited incomes and assets who can progress faster and lead the way for the less fortunate? Should one focus on the dense concentrations of poverty that exist in urban areas, or on providing new opportunities for rural areas in order to stem the urban drift that causes these concentrations? Should one make a special effort to focus on women who are normally the most disadvantaged within poor communities and households, and who often have the greatest potential for contributing to development? It is easy to say that AT should be aimed at the mass of the poor, but difficult to decide what parts of that mass are most deserving of assistance.

Which technologies?

AT interventions aim to ensure that the poor have greater access to the basic goods and services which will improve the quality of their lives. These normally include: food; clothing; essential household commodities such as stoves, pots and soap; water supplies; sanitation; basic health, education, transport, energy and communication facilities.

How can one compare the values of these different AT areas and how can one choose priority areas for intervention? Should production of food and clothing be given more emphasis than provision of shelter? Should emphasis be placed on helping subsistence farmers to grow more food or helping the landless to earn income through the production of basic goods, so that they can buy more food? Should provision of basic infrastructural facilities come first or should interventions aim at

95

providing employment opportunities for the poor in the processing of food, the manufacture of building materials and the building of roads, so that they themselves can help to finance the improvement of their own communities?

Priorities cannot be decided for the poor, who must be carefully consulted about their own priorities. AT interventions which seek to introduce technologies which are not perceived by the intended beneficiaries as a priority need are doomed to failure. Care needs to be taken to include all members of a community (especially the women) in the consultation process, and assistance should be given in helping communities to consider all the implications of the various options open to them.

Group 2: Alternative approaches to the introduction of AT

There are two main routes through which a viable AT can be introduced and disseminated. These are:

o *the extension route*, which relies heavily on governmental and other extension workers to spread information on new tools and techniques and to distribute improved goods and equipment or spread improved techniques through training;
o *the commercial route* which relies on normal market channels to establish the production of a new technology and to promote its distribution to large numbers of people.

Consideration needs to be given to the advantages and disadvantages of each approach, and dissemination strategies planned accordingly. The most appropriate routes for dissemination may depend on the technology involved. Often a combination of elements of both routes may be called for.

The extension route

Dissemination of technology through extension services can be advantageous in situations where there are large numbers of people who have no cash and no assets (except their labour) and where the technology involved is unlikely to yield increases in income which could attract and help to pay off loans. This route is often associated with heavy subsidization and 'hand-outs', and with the mobilization of poor people to do things for themselves on a self-help basis. Disadvantages with this approach are that it is very resource-intensive and the expense involved prevents large numbers of people being reached within a reasonable time-frame. Remote communities inevitably lose out. Attempts to augment coverage by training a few farmers or artisans in

96

the hope that they will train others normally fail. Water systems or other infrastructural facilities which are installed free often fall into disrepair through lack of community involvement and commitment.

The commercial route
If appropriate technologies such as improved stoves, efficient brick-moulding presses and improved farm tools are to reach the millions of poor people who could benefit from their use, then commercial channels will almost certainly need to be utilized. An obvious danger with this approach is that it can exclude people who have no access to cash. For this reason, it is important that schemes which provide consumer and producer credit to the rural and urban poor are established. Small-scale decentralized production of goods and equipment can help to ensure a local source of user training and after-sales service. Failing this, extension channels may be needed to train people how to use the new technologies and to repair the equipment. Since new technologies are involved, an extension phase will often need to be planned as a way of encouraging commercial forces to come into play. This will involve convincing potential consumers that they wish to buy the new product or technology and demonstrating to potential producers that a market exists for it.

Governments and other institutions play a critical role in both approaches. In the former approach, their extension personnel and technical and financial resources (often supplied through development assistance programmes) are the main way in which farmers and artisans receive water systems, roads, schools, clinics and public health education. In the latter approach, government support is necessary to provide a policy environment and institutional structure which favours the small decentralized enterprises which are the social carriers of most appropriate technologies.

Group 3: The effects and impact of Appropriate Technology — who benefits?
Different people are affected in different ways by the introduction and dissemination of new technologies and techniques. Inevitably, some people gain while others lose. It is important to think about how different groups of people will be affected over time so that an assessment can be made of the net worth of a project.

Issues which need to be addressed include:

o Will the rich members of societies benefit at the expense of poorer members, because of their greater access to land, cash, credit, education, transport facilities, etc?

97

o Will some poor members of society benefit at the expense of others, through for instance the displacement of some artisanal producers owing to the introduction of improved technologies to others in the same trade?

o Will men within a household benefit at the expense of the women and children through concentrating the means of earning income in the hands of the former or increasing the burden of unpaid work of the latter?

o Will consumers benefit at the expense of producers through, for instance, the introduction of cheap mass-produced basic goods which put thousands of small rural producers out of work?

o Will today's poor people benefit at the expense of tomorrow's through, for instance, the proliferation of income-generating opportunities which increase the rate of depletion of natural resources such as forests and soil or increase the extent of pollution?

In planning projects for the introduction of AT, thought needs to be given to measures which will be necessary to ensure that the poor benefit as well as the rich, that women benefit as well as men and that the livelihoods of future generations are considered as well as those alive today. Sometimes, it may be impossible to assist one vulnerable group of people without having a negative effect on others. In these cases, measures need to be planned which will provide adequate compensation to those who are harmed by the introduction and use of the new technology. A long-term view should be taken in planning AT projects. It is easy to confuse means with ends, and to concentrate on short-term responses to immediate problems without addressing the more serious, long-term development needs of a community. Project planning should look past the initial requirements for developing, testing, and demonstrating a technology to the more distant and difficult needs to be met in providing for its widespread use. Planners should look not only at the initial community or group selected for pilot activity, but also at the larger society that could use the technology, and adapt technology design and development to meet its needs. It is easy to pick out the most capable, best endowed groups in order to achieve pilot project successes ('effects'), but it is far more difficult to serve the needs and have an *impact* on the welfare of the bulk of the rural poor — unless one considers the limitations and the aspirations of this group from the project's beginnings.

The difference between effects and impact is also important in the evaluation of AT projects. Most evaluations take place at the project's conclusion, at which time the effects of the AT intervention — installation of new technologies, completion of training programmes, etc — are fairly clear. However, the impact of the project, whether or not it will increase rural production and incomes, is rarely evident at this time. It may be several years after the project team has ceased to work before an accurate appraisal of impact can be made. However, by this time, most organizations have turned their attentions elsewhere. They do not learn whether the rural poor are benefitting from AT — whether production increased; whether that increase was translated into rural income or absorbed as increased profits for distributors or savings for urban consumers; whether the bulk of the poor for whom the technology was intended were actually able to acquire and use it, or if it became largely the property of higher income groups; and most important, whether the technology served to improve the quality of life in rural areas, and to reduce the gaps between rural and urban standards, as well as the massive migration to cities caused by this gap.

Group 4: Institutions and AT
From an institutional standpoint, two major issues arise:

o What type of organization (and individual) can help in implementing AT programmes, and what are the strengths and weaknesses of each?
o What institutional arrangements can be made to combine the strengths of some or all of these groups into the service of AT generation and dissemination.

Simply put: who is best at doing what, and how can they all be brought together?

Institutions. Many types of institution (and individual) have been involved in AT programmes:

o *Research institutes and universities.* Whether located in developed or developing countries, these can be excellent sources of knowledge and invention. However, their refined environment can at times distance them from the needs and capabilities of the rural poor.
o *Commercial companies.* These are also a source of invention in developing countries. In addition, they can play a crucial role in the commercial production and distribution of appropriate technologies. Commercial companies in developed countries can also play a part in the development and dissemination of appropriate technologies in the Third World if it is in their financial interest to do so.
o *Local farmers, artisans and retailers (particularly women).* Who, for the most part, are the social carriers and projected beneficiaries of appropriate technology? These people often have much knowledge and skill to contribute to AT development and dissemination. All

99

too often, however, they are not consulted or enabled to participate in the process because of poor communications and institutional barriers to their participation.

○ *Central and regional government agencies*. These possess vast resources of buildings, transport, equipment and extension personnel that can support the development of AT from initial trials to widespread dissemination. These bodies are also essential in creating a policy environment which is conducive to the growth of small-scale industry and the spread of appropriate technologies.

○ *Commercial banks and development finance institutions*. These can provide the fixed and working capital essential for the promotion of AT activities. Often, their standard financing methods and appraisal techniques cannot accommodate the specific needs and conditions of small, decentralized rural enterprises, village artisans or women's groups. In many countries, however, innovative rural credit schemes have been successfully introduced.

○ *Local non-Government organizations*. These are normally very sensitive to the needs of the rural poor and have a good understanding of the type of assistance measures which are most beneficial. Unfortunately, they often lack sufficient technical or commercial competence, or financial resources, to sustain AT projects or to replicate their work beyond a small area.

○ *International donors and technical assistance agencies*. These can provide essential funds and necessary specialist expertise for AT programmes in developing countries. Such assistance is most likely to benefit the rural poor if necessary care is taken to consult and work with those local organizations which understand local needs and conditions. Although international agencies can play a useful role in helping to establish a local technical capability, they often promote technological dependency instead.

Institutional framework: Successful AT development and dissemination requires bringing the strengths of all these various agencies together, helping to overcome their weaknesses, and establishing new institutional relationships when necessary. Important factors which need consideration include:

○ criteria for choosing a focus agency which can co-ordinate all the various inputs and the methods by which this co-ordination can be achieved and maintained;

○ methods for implementing a truly collaborative approach to development, whereby knowledge travels up from the rural poor to the development agency, and international agencies learn from local agencies, as well as the other way round.

Group 5: Implications arising from the development and transfer of technologies

Can the needs of the poor in developing countries be served best by transferring technologies from overseas? Or is it better for each country to have its own capacity to generate appropriate technologies? Should development assistance concentrate on transferring technologies or on building up indigenous technical capacity?

Technology transfer

It is tempting to try and meet pressing needs in developing nations by importing hardware. This can be put into service upon arrival, and in the short term might satisfy some of these needs. Certainly such importing provides a more immediate solution than the time-consuming process of developing local capacity to produce hardware to serve the same purpose. However, it is not often a long-term solution, and it can even create new problems through the establishment of a dependency within the country upon external supplies and knowledge. Machines which require imported spare parts, fuel, or service technicians soon cease to produce at optimum levels, and donors who are willing to put up the initial purchase funds for imported equipment are usually much less willing to assist in financing the recurrent costs which its continued use involves.

Indigenous technical capacity

By definition, a technology which is appropriate in one place, and one set of conditions, will not be appropriate in another. Technologies have to be adapted to the individual environments and needs of communities. Therefore, even if a developing country is relying on imported technologies, it will still need the internal capacity to adapt this to local circumstances. Ideally, each country should have the capacity to adapt technologies in use elsewhere and to upgrade those traditional technologies being used within its own borders.

Although a local capacity to adapt and generate technologies is more likely to come up with appropriate products and processes than is a foreign research institute, results can still be poor if design and development work is done in isolation in an urban laboratory. Local scientists and engineers may have a good idea of what can be done in a given technical field, but may have as little knowledge as foreign technologists about the limitations presented in particular communities. People living in these communities usually have an excellent understanding of their environment and what it can and cannot support, but incomplete knowledge of the materials and techniques that are available to address their needs. Many projects put scientists to work on local problems, but few make use of local expertise. The key to AT development probably lies in blending this indigenous and external knowledge.

Indigenous knowledge is difficult to utilize if AT design work takes place outside of the community where it is intended for use. Local cultivating, manufacturing, and marketing skills should be drawn upon from the first stages of technology development, not just in the latter stages of testing. Much AT intended for widespread production and use never achieves that status because it did not take account of the capabilities and needs of local producers and users when it was designed. The R & D process for AT should maximize the participation of local artisans, farmers, distributors, and particularly local women, who are the main users of the technologies.

Appendix 2   Speakers and participants

Tor Halfdan Asse   Rogaland Research Institute
Iftikar Ahmed   ILO
Roger Andersson   Hifab International A/S
Harald Arvesen   The Export Council of Norway
Bård Aspen   Norwegian Water Resources and Electricity Board
Johan Bakken   Audio-Light A/S
Jon Berg   Directorate of Public Roads
Kjersti Berre   The Royal Norwegian Ministry of Development
   Co-operation (MDC)
Terje Bodøgaard   Architect
Theodor Borchgrevink   Directorate of Public Roads
Tor Brattvåg   COMPUTAS A/S
Live Brekke   NORCONSULT A/S
Arild Broch   NORPLAN A/S
Roar Brynlund   TELEPLAN A/S
Marilyn Carr   ITDG
Olav Dugstad   Electricity Bureau NETCOM
Sissel Ekås   The Royal Norwegian Ministry of Development
   Co-operation (MDC)
Turid H. Eriksen   The Royal Norwegian Ministry of Development
   Co-operation (MDC)
Michael Fergus   NORPLAN A/S
Erling Fosser   ORGUT A/S
Matthews. Gamser   ITDG
Tore Gjøs   Directorate of Public Roads
Brian Glover   NORPLAN A/S
Øystein Glømmi   The Royal Norwegian Ministry of Development
   Co-operation (MDC)
Gisle Kvaal Grebstad   NOTEBY A/S
Geir Grinde   Abrahamsen & Grinde
Ole-J. Hafsten   NORPLAN A/S
Ragnar Hansen   INTERCONSULT A/S
Torstein Herfjord   Norwegian Water Resources and Electricity
   Board
John Hermansen   Norwegian Institute of Technology
Erik Hestnes   Norwegian Geotechnical Institute
Paul Hofseth   The Royal Norwegian Ministry of Environment
Sven A. Holmsen   The Royal Norwegian Minsitry of Development
   Co-operation (MDC)
Astrid Holte   Fylkesmannen i Hordaland
John Howe   IT Transport

Frits N. Jensen   NORPLAN A/S
Torodd Jensen   Norwegian Water Resources and Electricity Board
Fritz Johansen   Norwegian Hydrodynamic Laboratory
Tore Johansen   NORPLAN A/S
Knut Kaiser   The Royal Norwegian Ministry of Development
   Co-operation (MDC)
Gaim Kebreab   Norwegian Church Aid
Francis Kifukwe   NORCONSULT A/S
Helge Kjekshus   The Royal Norwegian Ministry of Development
   Co-operation (MDC)
Svein Kopperud   Taugbol & Øverland A/S
Trygve Kropelien   KENOR A/S
Axel Lasson   Norwegian Institute of Technology
Henning Lauridzen   Institute of Transport Economics
Geir Lenes   NOTEBY A/S
Gunnar Lerdal   SAPI STRONGPACK A/S
Øystein Linge   Norwegian Telephone Company
Tore Lium   Hifab International A/S
Stein Lundeby   NORCONSULT A/S
Leif-Egil Lørum   NORCONSULT A/S
Bjørn Martens   Ing. Kjell Bruer A/S
George McRobie   ITDG
Marit Melhuus   Institute of Social Anthropology
Asbjørn Moe   Bærum Electricity Board
Dipak Nandy   ITDG
Bjørn Gustav Nielsen   Electricity Bureau A/S
Dolf Noppen   NORCONSULT A/S
Liv Nordbye   Taugbøl & Øverland A/S
Svein Georg Nyblin   Norwegian Society of Chartered Engineers
Kenneth Riley   NORPLAN A/S
Aksel Roksti   NORPLAN A/S
Jan A. Roti   NOTEBY A/S
Marit Roti   The Royal Norwegian Ministry of Development
   Co-operation (MDC)
Olav Werner Ruud   Directorate of Public Roads
Tore Roy Semb   Ing. Chr. F. Grøner A/S
Henrik Sevaldsen   TELEPLAN
Ole Salomonsen   Bodø Housing Cooperation
Terje Simensen   Norwegian Institute of Technology
Mark Sinclair   ITDG
Eivind Skaug   Directorate of Public Roads
Steinar Skjæveland   The Royal Norwegian Ministry of Development
   Co-operation (MDC)
Egil Skofteland   Norwegian Water Resources and Electricity Board

Rolf Skudal   The Royal Norwegian Ministry of Development
    Co-operation (MDC)
Eli Sletten   The Royal Norwegian Ministry of Development
    Co-operation (MDC)
Magne Solgaard   INTERCONSULT A/S
Kjell K. Svendsen   Ing. Chr. Grøner A/S
Jan Erik Sørlie   NOTEBY A/S
Kjell Ivar Tangen   Norwegian Telephone Company
Stein Torbjørnsen   NORCONSULT A/S
Jan Ulleberg   Taugbøl & Øverland A/S
Velsa Vetlesen   The Royal Norwegian Ministry of Development
    Co-operation (MDC)
Clifford Wang   NORCONSULT A/S
John White   OECD
Fredrik Ystehede   NORCONSULT A/S
Jon R. Ivarson Øgland   NIPA

Notes and references

Technologies for developing countries: George McRobie

1. Sinclair, A., *A Guide to AT Institutions*, IT Publications, London, 1984.

2. Carr, M., *The AT Reader*, IT Publications, London, England, 1985.

3. Fricke, T., 'High Impact Appropriate Technology Case Studies', AT International, Washington, 1983.

4. Stewart, F., ed., *Macro-Policies and Appropriate Technology*, Westview Press, Colorado, 1987.

5. In India, there is the Institute of Rural Management, Anand, a centre of outstanding quality; the Indian Institutes of Technology in Delhi and Bombay, and the Khadi and Village Industries Commission, among others; the University of Science and Technology, Ghana, and the University of Dar Es Salaam, Tanzania; the Postgraduate College, Chapingo, Mexico, and the Institute of Technology, Costa Rica; the National Altiplano University, Puno, and the Catholic University, Lima, Peru; the Asian Institute of Technology and the universities of Kasetsart and Khon Kaen, Thailand; and the Bandung Institute of Technology, Indonesia.

Aid and Appropriate Technology: John White

1. Fred Fluitman and John White, 'External Development Finance and Choice of Technology', World Employment Programme Research, Working Paper WEP 2–22/WP 81, ILO, 1981; and Jeffrey James and Susumu Watanabe (eds.), *Technology, Institutions and Government Policies*, Macmillan Series of ILO Studies, Macmillan, 1985, Chapter 7.

2. 'DAC Guidelines on Local and Recurrent Cost Financing', published as Annex III in *Development Co-operation: Efforts and Policies of the Members of the Development Assistance Committee: 1979 Review*, OECD, 1979.

3. See 'Good Procurement Practices for Official Development Assistance', Annex I of *Development Co-operation: Efforts and Policies of the members of the Development Assistance Committee: 1986 Review*, OECD, 1987.

4. Robert Cassen and Associates, *Does Aid Work?*, Oxford University Press, 1986, Chapter 5.

5. The term 'evangelist' is used here in its secondary technical sense, signifying 'an itinerant preacher having no fixed pastoral charge' (*Oxford English Dictionary*). Any meliorative or pejorative connotation is unintended.

106

6. The progress made a few years ago on the financing of local and recurrent costs is noted in an earlier paragraph (see note 2). The present climate favours international competitive bidding, which tends to aggregate procurement into blocks from which local suppliers are largely excluded (see note 3; see also earlier work by UNITAR on alternative procurement methods).

7. Cassen, op.cit, pp. 191–2.

Gender, culture and Appropriate Technology: Marit Melhuus

1. Herbst, Philip; 1974. 'The Product of work is people', *Sociotechnical Designs*, Tavistock, London.

2. This feat is accomplished in an astounding variety of ways. The past decade has yielded an enormous amount of ethnographic and theoretical literature documenting women's situation and confronting the epistemological problems that the issue of gender gives rise to. See, for example:

Afshar, Haleh (ed.); 1985. *Women, work and ideology in the Third World.* Tavistock, London.

Barker, D.L. and Allen, Sheila; 1976. *Dependence and Exploitation in Work and Marriage.* Longman, London.

Berk, Sarah Fenstermaker; 1980. *Women and household labour.* Sage, London.

The Cambridge Women's Study Group; 1981. *Women in society: interdisciplinary essays.* Virago, London.

Cutrufelli, Maria Rosa; 1983. *Women of Africa: Roots of oppression.* Zed Press, London.

Leacock, Eleanor B; 1981. *Myths of male dominance: collected articles on women cross-culturally.* Monthly Review Press, New York.

Long, Norman (ed.); 1984. *Family and work in rural societies: Perspectives on non-wage labour.* Tavistock Publ., London.

Reiter, Rayna R. (ed.); 1975. *Towards an anthropology of women.* Monthly Review Press, New York.

Rogers, Barbara; 1980. *The Domestication of women: Discrimination in developing societies.* Tavistock, London.

UNESCO; 1984. *Women on the move: Contemporary changes in family and society.* UNESCO, Paris.

Young, Kate; Wolkowitz, Carol; McCullogh, Roslyn (eds.); 1981. *Of marriage and the market: Women's subordination in international perspective.* CSE Books, London.

3. In October 1986, Jorun Solheim, Tordis Borchgrevink and myself drafted a presentation of the issue 'Gender at Work' for a seminar in preparation of the 'Thorsrud Memorial Symposium'. As some of our mutual ideas are reflected in this article, I wish to acknowledge this collective effort, through taking sole responsibility for the resetting of the theme.

4. See Melhuus, M. and Borchgrevink, T. (1984) 'Husarbeid — tids

binding av kvinner', I. Rudie (ed.) *Myk start — Hard landing.* Universitetsforlaget, Oslo.

5. See Sharp, Lauriston. 1952. 'Steel axes for Stone Age Australians'. *Human organization.* Vol. II (Bobbs Merrill Reprint).

6. See Archetti, E.P. 1985. 'Cultural Change and Development'. Institute of Social Anthropology, University of Oslo.

7. Vanek presents these figures for American housewives: 55 hours per week for the full-time housewife and 26 hours per week for the employed wife. Vanek, J. 1974. 'Time spent in housework'. *Scientific American.* Vol. V. For Norway the figures in 1971–2 were 51.8 hours for the full-time housewife and 30.8 for the employed wife. (NOU. Tidsnytting-sundersøkelsen 1971–2). Oakley gives a figure of 77 hours per week spent on housework for English housewives, but no data are given for employed wives. Oakley, A.; 1974. *Sociology of housework.* Pantheon Books, N.Y.

8. I realize that I have not answered the question of *why* women continue to invest so much time in housework. This has been treated elsewhere (see e.g. Melhuus, M. and Borchgrevink, T., op.cit.)

9. This case is based on a study carried out by Eduardo Archetti for the Ministry of Agriculture in Ecuador in 1984.

10. Obviously, at this point this topic is too broad to go into, but I am convinced that it is paramount not only to take into account women's work, but also the whole domestic unit (whether a production unit or not) by considering it a decision-making unit i.e. an active agent and not just a passive receptor of development, whose decisions not only effect the private sphere but in fact have an impact on the public arenas (e.g. decisions to migrate.)

A basic needs strategy: Iftikhar Ahmed
Notes

1. It is interesting that many of the fast-growing (per capita GNP of 2.5 per cent per annum) African countries (notably Nigeria and Côte d'Ivoire) were poor in basic needs' achievements (Table 1). Not all the African countries experiencing a negative growth performed poorly in basic needs' achievements (see Madagascar and Zambia, and even Zaire despite being constrained by very low per capita income).

2. An all-purpose primitive jungle knife.

3. The 'dhenki' is a foot-operated wooden husker.

4. The effects of the fall in the price of capital is reinforced by low tariffs on imports (Government of Bangladesh, 1985, p.109).

5. This section draws heavily from Hussain and Aziz, 1981.

6. This section is based on Carla Risseeuw, 1980.

7. The biogas plant can be used for heating, lighting, power irrigation pumps or generating electrical power for local use. In addition, it makes an excellent fertilizer and the sludgelike residue that is left behind after the fermentation process contains all of the nitrogen, phosphorous and potassium of the original material.

8. The Gobar Gas and Agricultural Machinery Development Company which produces these is located at Butwal in Rapandebi district.

References

Abdullah; Taherunnesa, 'Women in rice farming systems in Bangladesh and how technology programmes can reach them' in *Women in rice farming*, Gower, Aldershot, 1985.

Ahmad, Q.K., *Promotion of employment and income through rural non-crop activities in Bangladesh*, Research Report No.45, Dhaka, Bangladesh Institute of Development Studies, Dhaka, March 1986a.

Ahmad, Q.K., 'Appropriate technology in rural industrial development in South Asia', paper presented at the meeting of the Committee on Studies for Co-operation in Development in South Asia, Dhaka 23–4 September, Bangladesh Institute of Development Studies, Dhaka, 1986b.

Ahmad, Q.K., 'Female employment in Bangladesh: a review of status and policy', *UN decade for women 1976–85: situation of women in Bangladesh*, Ministry of Social Welfare and Women's Affairs, Government of Bangladesh, Dhaka, May 1985.

Ahmad, Q.K. and Islam, Rafiqul, *Rice husking: a comparative study of different methods*, Studies on Rural Industries Development (Dhaka, Bangladesh Institute of Development Studies, October 1984).

Ahmed, Iftikhar, 'Technology, production linkages and women's employment in south Asia', *International Labour Review*, Vol.126, No.1, Jan.– Feb. 1987.

Ahmed, Iftikhar, 'Rural technologies and women: an ILO project in Ghana', *Women at Work* (ILO, Geneva), No.2, 1986.

Ahmed, Iftikhar, *Technology and rural women: conceptual and empirical issues*, Allen and Unwin, London, 1985.

Ahmed, Iftikhar, and Kinsey, Bill H., *Farm equipment innovations in eastern and central southern Africa* Gower, Aldershot, 1984.

Ahmed, J.U., 'The impact of new paddy post-harvest technology on the rural poor in Bangladesh' in Martin Greeley and Michael Howes (eds.): *Rural technology, rural institutions and the rural poorest*, Dhaka, Comilla, Bangladesh, Centre on Integrated Rural Development for Asia and the Pacific; Institute of Development Studies, Brighton, Sussex, 1982.

Appropriate Technology Development Organisation (ATDO), *Biogas technology*, Islamabad, Pakistan, ATDO, undated.

Arnold, J.E.M., 'Wood energy and rural communities', paper presented at the *Eighth World Forestry Congress*, Jakarta, October 1978, FAO, Rome, 1978.

Batliwala, Srilatha, 'Rural energy scarcity and nutrition: a new perspective' in *Economic and Political Weekly*, Vol.17, No.9, 27 February 1982.

Batliwala, Srilatha, 'Women and cooking energy' in *Economic and Political Weekly*, Vol.XVIII, Nos.52 and 53, December 24–31 1983.

Cain, M.L., 'Java, Indonesia: the introduction of rice processing technology' in R. Dauber and M.L. Cain (eds.): *Women and technological change in developing countries*, Westview Press, Boulder, 1981.

Carr, M., 'Technologies for rural women: impact and dissemination' in I. Ahmed (ed.), *Technology and rural women: conceptual and empirical issues* Allen and Unwin, London, 1985.

Collier, William L., Sinhardi, J. Colter, and d'A Shaw, Robert: *Choice of technique in rice milling in Java: a comment*, Research and Training Network, (Agricultural Development, Council, New York, September 1974), reprint.

ESCAP, *Participation of women in dairy development in South Asia*, ST/ESCAP/171, ESCAP, Bangkok, 1981.

Ghai, Dharam, 'Successes and failures in African development: 1960–82', paper presented at the seminar on 'Alternative Development Strategies', Development Centre, Organisation for Economic Co-operation and Development, Paris, 28–30 January 1987.

Government of Bangladesh: *The Third Five Year Plan: 1985–90*, Planning Commission, Dhaka, December 1985.

Grameen Bank: *Grameen Bank annual report 1984* Grameen Bank Head Office, Khaka, 1985.

Gulati, Leela, 'Fisherwomen on the Kerala coast', *Women, Work and Development 8*, ILO, Geneva, 1984a.

Gulati, Leela, 'Technological change and women's behaviour: a case study of three fishing villages', *Economic and Political Weekly*, Vol. XIX, No.49, 8 December 1984b.

Hussain, Syeda Abida, and Aziz, Faizia, 'The Shah Jewna dairy project in Pakistan' in *Participation of women in dairy development*, ESCAP, Bangkok, 1981.

ILO, *Employment expansion through rural industrialisation in Bangladesh: potentials, problems and policy issues* ARTEP, Bangkok, 1985.

ILO/ARTEP, *Fighting poverty: Asia's major challenge*, ILO/Asian Regional Team for Employment Promotion, New Delhi, 1986.

ILO/FAO, *Report of joint inter-agency mission on the preparatory work the establishment of an African regional network for agricultural tools and equipment*, Geneva/Rome, 1985.

ILO/Ghana National Council on Women and Development, *Technologies for rural women — Ghana*, Technical Manual Series Nos.1–5, fish smoking, cassava processing, palm-oil processing, coconut oil processing and soap manufacturing, Accra, 1985–7.

ILO/Norway, *Technological change, basic needs and the condition of rural women*, Report of the joint ILO/Government of Norway African Regional Project ILO/NOR/78/RAF/27, Geneva, 1984.

ILO/Philippine Bureau of Forest Development, *Implementation of appropriate technology in Philippine forestry*, Manila, 1982.

Khoju, M.J., *Commercial application of new indigenous technologies: a case study of Nepal*, ILO World Employment Programme mimeographed research working paper, Geneva, 1984.

Laarman, J., Virtamen, K., and Jurvelius, M., *Choice of technology in forestry: a Philippine case study* New Day Publishers for the ILO, Quezon City, Philippines, 1981.

Ligunya, Alice A., 'Rural women from developing countries in energy technologies' in *Women challenge technology*, Vol.II, University of Aalborg, Aalborg, Denmark, 1986.

Mies, Maria, 'Indian women in subsistence and agricultural labour', *Women, Work and Development 12*, ILO, Geneva, 1986.

Risseeuw, Carla, *The wrong end of the rope: women coir workers in Sri Lanka* (Leiden/Colombo, 1980).

Salahuddin, Khaleda, *Impact of technological change in agriculture on rural women of Bangladesh*, Dhaka, Polwel Printing Press, 1986.

Singer, Hans, *Technologies for basic needs*, ILO, Geneva, 1979.

Srivastava, J.C., 'Harvesting technology for eliminating the drudgery of women engaged in rice production, processing and utilisation' in *Women in rice farming*, Gower, Aldershot, 1985.

Tinker, I., 'New technologies for food-related activities: an equity strategy' in Dauber and Cain, op.cit.

Tucker, J.B., 'Biogas systems in India: is the technology appropriate? in *Development Digest*, Vol.XXI, No.1, July 1983.

Institutional aspects of Appropriate Technology: Marilyn Carr

1. See for example R. Chambers, *Rural Development: Putting the Last First* (Longman, 1983).

2. This was one of the ideas which ITDG had in mind when it promoted the establishment of national AT Centres during the 1960s and 1970s. For a list of such Centres see ITDG's *Appropriate Technology Institutions: A Directory*, (IT Publications, London, Revised edition, 1985).

3. For description of the work of these and other AT institutions see Angela Sinclair, *A Guide to Appropriate Technology Institutions* (IT Publications, London, 1985).

4. For an interesting description of this experience see Smillie, I., *No Condition Permanent: Pump Priming Ghana's Industrial Revolution* (IT Publications, London, 1986).

5. Opole, M., 'The Kenya ceramic jiko stove', *Sustainable Industrial Development*, Ed. Carr, M., IT Publications, London, 1988.

6. Hislop, D. 'The micro-hydro programme in Nepal — a case study' *Sustainable Industrial Development*, Ed. Carr, M., IT Publications, London, 1988.

7. Hislop, D., op.cit.

8. Akerele, D., *Traditional palm oil processing, women's role and the application of appropriate technology* (ECA/ATRCW, Addis Ababa, 1985).

9. This subject is covered in detail in this volume by John White's 'Aid and Appropriate Technology: multilateral and bilateral programmes'.